CREATE
AND
CELEBRATE!

JAY C. ROCHELLE

FORTRESS PRESS
PHILADELPHIA

Library of Congress Catalog Card Number 79–139345

ISBN 0–8006–0016–9

Printed in the United States of America

3403E72   1–16

What's Inside

Preface

This book arose out of need. A number of people have contacted me over the past years seeking help in making worship meaningful. I have a limited but useful reputation as a liturgical innovator, and I have been acquainted with new forms of worship through both reading and experience since the early 1960s.

In my conversations, I've found that many people don't know why they want to experiment with new forms of worship. I've tried to write for them the reasons they cannot find the words to express; I only hope my words will ring true for them. This book is offered as a resource tool for youth groups and congregational worship committees. I hope young people can buy what I'm saying because I've had my best experiences with them. Maybe this book is in payment of a debt of gratitude.

The simplest details of a service become a problem for the congregation which has never tackled new forms of worship. That is the reason for chapter 3, a "do-it-yourself" chapter. The beginning chapters deal with why you should do it yourself. The material in chapter 3 comes from the requests for help I've received. Modern worship forms are still a mystery to many congregations of all traditions, and this material may help you to avoid the pitfalls in what ought to be a good experience.

This book is deliberately short in order to be readable. It gives enough material to start you in the right direction. It is not definitive. It does not have all of the "right answers." It wasn't meant to.

A word of caution. Whoever reads this book and buys its contents without pushing them through his own mind will end up only by reproducing *my* thing. I don't want that. My interest is in more congregations (and especially the young people, whom I love so much) learning enough to be able to do *their* thing. Some people have the ability to do this without help. But most of us need a little help from our friends. I wish I had had a book like this when I broke into new patterns of worship. I can only offer it in that spirit.

My thanks to Clint Miller for the original scoring of the music for the Christmas Folk Mass, to Conrad Weiser for arrangements, and to my friends of Saint John's for their participation.

1

Why Bother?

In lots of corners of the church many people are asking the question, Is worship possible anymore? Is preaching doing anything? What does it mean to worship in the Christian church? This book is meant to give pointers toward creative worship experiences. The whole book rests on the belief that there are real possibilities for worship in the late twentieth century. So rather than sidestep the issue, we'd better confront it right away.

Let's begin at ground zero. Let us assume that there is no shape to our knowledge of God. We aren't sure if God exists; we aren't sure who or what he might be; we may feel simply a "God-shaped blank" at the center of our lives. Let us assume that we haven't much knowledge about God, and that the knowledge we do have leaves us indifferent.

Suppose, now, it were possible to find God in some concrete way. Suppose God would reveal himself to man in a form which would be recognizable, tangible; a form to which man could relate. Let us suppose that it were possible for God to become man! Crazy thought!

In point of fact, however, Christianity rises and falls with its faith that this is precisely what did happen in history, and continues to happen! There was a man named Jesus, from Nazareth. People communicated with him; he communicated with people, especially those on whom institutional religion had given up: tax collectors, prostitutes, drunks. He had a magnetic personality. He had charisma. His teaching and preaching polarized people. There seemed to be no middle ground available when he came to you. Either you hated him or you loved him. He didn't seem to be threatened by this. Not that he was without feeling! He was a man of intense feeling. But he had made his peace with himself, and he knew how people would react to him. He warned a few people not to follow him, that the road was too steep for them. Others he gathered to his side. He said something about sowing the word and letting the soil grow crops where it could. He left a great deal to the imagination; in fact, most of his appeal was to the imagination, the emotions, and the common knowledge of men. He spoke of birdlife, of sowing and reaping, of large barns, of different kinds of seeds, thus appealing to common knowledge in an agrarian society.

Mostly he spoke about the kingdom of God. He never defined the kingdom of God, except through pictures and symbolic healings. These pictures (called parables) and symbolic healings (called miracles) were really flashes of light on the kingdom of God. Those who saw the meaning of the parables and miracles understood that the kingdom of God was right by their sides. It was the "place" where God ruled in the hearts of men; it was the "place" where the healing of man's physical, spiritual, and emotional conditions was happening, where men were becoming whole; it was the "place" where the future no longer held fear but promise and joy; the "place" where hope determined the style of life,

and love shaped all relationships among people. It was
—and is—the most beautiful "place" in the world.

In the end he was put to death. He could see it
coming. He polarized too many people. He shook the
foundations of the religious establishment with a very
free form of religion; he made the civil authorities nervous with his call to total and final allegiance to the
kingdom of God. He spoke of love in a world satisfied
with hate.

Then the strangest thing happened! "On the third
day he rose again, according to the Scriptures." The
people who had responded to him saw him anew in their
community life. He was known in the interpretation of
the Scriptures, in the breaking of bread, and in the love
of the community one for another. Rooms, countries,
continents—none could any longer contain him. His life
had been vindicated by a Power beyond man.

Exhilarated but shaken by their experience of Christ
and the God beyond and within him, the growing group
of people who saw his meaning for life began to speak
of him in terms usually reserved for high authorities
and for God himself. They called him "Lord"; they
called him "Son of God"; they began to speak of a deep
relationship between God the Father and Jesus (which
he himself had already indicated, but which they didn't
fully grasp until after the resurrection). By their experience of his freeing, loving presence in their lives,
they were eventually incapable of any other response
except to say that God is known in and through him.
It all sounded very blasphemous, but they were forced
into it. This way of talking was the only way they could
explain what a brand-new meaning he had given their

lives. The words they had were inadequate to the task, so they coined whole new vocabularies and gave old words new meanings to try to communicate the meaning of Christ.

Of course, to this day many have passed by Jesus the Christ, in search of another life-style by which to give meaning to their lives. There have, however, been many who have not walked on by and who have found in him a true centering of their lives; who have found in him a freedom which words fail fully to describe to those who do not know it (though this does not mean we give up trying to use words); who have found in him the pathway to joy and hope and peace in life. These are the people who worship. They do it, not because they have to, but because they want to. Jesus' message is an attitude, a mind-set, a style of life, that is best learned in community.

To worship means to attach worth or value to something. Whatever you attach the most worth to in your life—that becomes the center of your worship, whether you acknowledge it or not. The Christian is the one who attaches the final value in his life to Christ. Because of the liberation he has experienced in the cross and resurrection of Christ, he is able to say, "I want to give thanks to God for this freedom." Like the tenth leper, he has felt the touch of Christ and returns to give thanks to God. Thanksgiving is the name of the game; we often use a Greek word for it—*Eucharist*. But it means the same in any language. God has broken through to man in a big way, opening up life to new meaning, freeing us for service, creating out of the ashes of despair a new hope and joy in life. For that we give thanks!

There is more. We also worship because, by so doing, we are saying to the world—when we are serious about our worship life—that the preliminary things don't count in any final way. We are saying to the world that all the things on which the world generally centers its worship are not all they're cracked up to be! We are saying (if we are rich) that we are not going to be trapped by our wealth, deluded into relying on it for our "salvation," but we are going to press on through our wealth to God who is our salvation. We are saying (if we are well-educated) that an academic degree will not save us from the pitfalls of life; instead, we'll push on to God who has been there in the pitfalls of life and is still there with us. The worship life of the church says something to the world, however minimal that may be at times. Wherever something is really going on in worship, the world will get curious. It will want to know why we cannot be satisfied with wealth or education or progress or success or popularity as our gods; it will want to know why we've got to push on through all of these "means of grace" to some other God.

As we are able, we shall tell the world that we know a God who frees us and who does not sink hooks into us and trap us. We might say experience convinces us that to worship anything less than God-in-Christ spells shipwreck for man because all the lesser gods eventually cast man into bondage to themselves. Our God frees us for life and for service. We worship as a continual reminder and celebration of that fact. We might say, to take only one example, that really to worship education (even in a country which believes that education is the solution to many of its ills, and thus makes worship of education easy) will finally bind us into one narrow way of thinking. We will be so critical of and judgmental toward the uneducated man that we will no longer be able to see God at work in him—he will be a thing to us and not a person—and eventually we will find ourselves in bondage to this god of our own making. This god will mercilessly drive us to seek more and more education in order to fulfill the needs we've imagined for ourselves. For these reasons, we might tell the world, we press on beyond education to a God who frees us to love our brothers, educated and uneducated (though we wish the best in education for all men), a God whose only claim on us is that we accept ourselves because he has accepted us in the cross of Christ.

If we are historically conditioned, we might remind those who hit us with the question, Why do you Christians worship? that since its beginning Christianity has reserved God the Father and Jesus Christ the title *Lord.* We shall remind them that this means that the final allegiance in life is given, not to the state, not to the secular forms of salvation such as education or the idea of progress, but to the living Lord who does not enslave us but who frees us to be ourselves under him.

We also worship because this is a means of pointedly celebrating the presence of Christ in all of life. There is a recognizable danger in the lives of those who have "given up" on worship in a community experience such as the Sunday service. They may wind up worshiping nothing at all. Those who say they are able to worship God "in field and flower" have a point, in that God— if he is God—is present everywhere. But they will not receive much in the way of communication from God in the field. God communicates through his community. He speaks to us in the needs and in the words of others.

We receive his love when all the masks fall down, revealing people to others as they really are, and freeing them to love themselves and others. God set the style for this type of communication in Jesus of Nazareth; he has not, to anyone's knowledge, rescinded his plan. Christianity *is* community. It is continued through history in a community with some traditions and some historic consciousness. It has been said, and truly, that if you could remove all the signs of Christianity—church, Bible, sacraments, pastors—for a full generation, Christianity could not arise again. Unlike religious traditions which spring from the mystical reasoning of men, Christianity is based upon certain historical events, the loss of whose memory and power would spell the end of Christianity. Worship-in-community thus serves the function of *remembrance,* but remembrance for the purpose of shaping a life-style both now and in future. Christianity is not tied to traditionalism, but it is tied to "tradition," that is, to literature and symbols which explain the experience of Christ in the past in order to shape the present and future. Worship performs the specific job of recalling the meaning of the Christ-event for men in every age. Perhaps we can go one step further and speak of an effective presence of Christ in worship; that is, Christ really is in our midst in word and sacrament and community and once again frees us for life and love and hope. But here we crack up on words. We can only put up the signposts. This must become an *experience.*

If a person can experience Christ's presence in worship—in word, sacrament, and community—then all the foregoing statements make sense. They will not make sense to the person who wants to be satisfied with a spiritual idea of God. But to the person who suspects that Christianity is as much concerned with this life as the next, as much concerned about material reality as about spiritual reality, these statements will make eminent sense when proven in the crucible of experience.

I am convinced that the reason this experience is seldom felt is not a failure of worship itself, but a failure of the *modes* of worship. If we could break through the patterns of worship which negate our experience of life and of God, then we would again sense the loving, freeing, empowering presence of Christ in worship. The exciting possibility in all worship is that we *can* do this. It *has* been done. I have known many total experiences of worship, and I believe it is possible for the circle to grow wider. This is what the search for contemporary forms of worship is all about.

Conversations with young people reveal that for them the two most important aspects of Sunday's worship are the Absolution and the Eucharist. Here they can sense something happening in worship, no matter how clouded over it may be. Many young people identify with the opening confession and absolution, not because of the words (though the words may detract from it), but because they can sense acceptance of themselves with all their problems and unlovable characteristics. One beautiful high school junior told me that the reason Holy Communion was so meaningful for her was that she could feel a bond of love, and she had a feeling of being accepted for what she was, with no questions asked. This is an experience of worship!

Worship is intimately related to our whole pattern of life. This statement may appear to be untrue at first glance, but I want to show that it is true—to the best of my ability.

When we are dissatisfied with something in life—with our way of life or with some of the things we experience in the world around us—we say that we have become aware of a problem, an inconsistency, a gap between the world and what we as human beings are. All people who have feeling (and there is no one who is not a well of feeling; we have just been carefully taught not to show emotion, and thus to deny who we are!) recognize the binds of life. Most of the time we intellectualize the binds away and so rationalize the problem. But our condition is healthier if we confront our problems. In order to do that we must know who we are; we must know how far we can trust ourselves (particularly in interpersonal relationships); and as we learn to trust ourselves we automatically learn to trust others. My level oı trust in other people is a mirror of my level of trust in myself. At the same time all this is happening, our level of *awareness* rises. Having become aware of ourselves as persons, we are able to become aware of the problems that face or, perhaps, threaten us. We are challenged to respond by risking our knowledge and trust of ourselves in a concrete situation. Only in such a way can we continue to grow as people.

So the second step in the process is *confrontation*—meeting the problem head on with everything that you are and taking the chance that you will come to some kind of solution. The risk is high. You may fail! You may come off with no resolution to the problem. You may back off when you come to the true confrontation. You may be unable to put your whole life on the line.

Worship will never be possible if we cannot do this. If we cannot take this step (and none of us can take it alone) we shall never come to the point of liberation, of celebration.

To say that we cannot make the jump alone into confrontation with a problem means that there must be an arena of trust and love where we can deal with problems. When we know that there are those who believe in us as people, with all our faults and problems, and who trust us to confront a problem and come to a satisfactory conclusion, we are more capable of taking the risk. And to know this, in context, is to experience Christ in community. When we can come to each other with no masks, not hiding ourselves, and be accepted, we are freed to reach out continually and accept others —and to confront the problems of life. We are free to grow because the community has given us the strength to fill in our weaknesses, and loves us both in our weaknesses (which may prove to be our strengths) and in our strengths (which may prove to be our weaknesses). The circle of love must build out from two or three people who know and love and trust and accept each other at a deep level. This is the only way we can understand Jesus' saying, "wherever two or three are gathered together in my name, there am I in the midst of them." Alone, you can't be Christian—for the very simple reason that, alone, you can't be human.

With the community in us and with us and behind us, we are able to reach out—to take a risk—and meet problems head on. I'm not talking about problems that don't matter to us as persons, but problems that actually threaten our understanding of ourselves. To solve a

problem in tenth-grade algebra is hardly cause for celebration, unless (and it is possible) you are threatened
by your inability to solve it. In that case, the outcome
is a joyful liberation and a deeper trust in yourself which
leads again to the ability to take even greater risks as a
person.

So the third step, *commitment,* means that we were
challenged and found that we could rely on ourselves
in the situation. Or it means that we were challenged
and found that we could not rely on ourselves in the
situation. But there is cause for *celebration* even in the
midst of failure, when we see that the failure does not
destroy us as persons, but helps us to grow taller. In
order not to be destroyed by failure, we need the community of love and trust which does not reject us even
when we fail.

The outcome of the whole process is a sense of liberation, a sense of deeper self-trust and self-love which
leads to deeper trust and love for others, a sense of
being released. The only possible reaction this can bring
is "Thanks!" Which is the name of the game: Eucharist!
In the context of an emotional and intellectual worship experience, *Eucharist* means the spontaneous out-
burst of love and concern and trust and honesty that
spreads like wildfire through the whole community. It
means to be really alive!

Here the bankruptcy of words causes me to be quiet
again. I believe, however, that what I have just described
is the pattern of life and, further, that it is the pattern
of the worship life of the church. If we substitute for
celebration the word *worship,* we see where worship
fits into the total pattern of life (later we shall try to

show how the total pattern is the pattern of the worship
life of the church):

$$
\text{Community of love}
\begin{cases}
\text{Awareness (leads to)} \\
\text{Confrontation (leads to)} \\
\text{Commitment (leads to)} \\
\text{Celebration (leads to)} \\
\text{New Awareness . . . and so on.}
\end{cases}
$$

Worship continually frees us from the past to live in
the present in expectant hope for the future. We cannot
put it any other way. And the whole process is over-
arched by the community of love. Wherever you find one
person who loves you as you are, you have the basic
building block of life from which to build the bridges
into deep and joyful living.

The difficult thing is that of course such things cannot
be "taught." They must be understood in the crucible of
experience. I believe that the ability to be a community
of love is what gave the early Christian church its great
spirit and outreach. "See how these Christians love one
another!" The circle of love simply grew wider as people
turned to each other in a relationship of love, trust, concern, and honesty through their experience of Jesus
Christ. The type of "problem-solving" outlined in the
preceding pages is not a grim-faced approach to life
but an approach filled with joy and festivity, with gaiety
and a touch of mirth. The God whom we worship is
the God of joy, light, and life. This is his shape as
revealed in Christ. Perhaps what distinguishes the
Christian from other religious people is this hallmark
of joy and life even in the midst of trial ("problems"),
because the Christian is aware that all the problems of

life are taken up and transcended in the vision of hope which God has given us in the resurrection of Christ. This vision works itself out, practically speaking, in the fellowship of love, the community of trust, which is the worshiping/working church.

Probably the most we can expect from our worship life is that we will hit "highs" sometimes. We probably cannot live on the mountaintops at all times. If you sense in the word *probably* an underlying belief that we can, you are right. I do believe it is possible to live at peaks of worship, and we can strive for that possibility, in which festivity and life and love are all tied together in a bundle called worship. This belief is what gives drive to those people who are experimenting today with new forms of worship. It is a drive toward reality, not away from it. We must continually risk failure in order to achieve this kind of success—which leads us into chapter 2.

2

Kicking and Screaming
Our Way into Now

Why seek new forms of worship? The reason, put simply, is this: the old patterns, which once had universal validity and specific meaning in local situations, no longer possess their power, for large numbers of people. If worship is absolutely central to the Christian tradition (because it fits into the pattern of life, too!), then the church ought be working on worship patterns that make sense, not only in their use of current language, but also by relating to the needs of people. The bald truth is that our current patterns, despite much work in liturgical renewal, do not often meet people where they are. A period of long experimentation is necessary, to sink soundings into the needs of the people and the needs which ought be brought before God: the polarities which form the crucible of worship.

Most people no longer see the unity of the weekly worship service, which was once tuned in by the Propers (Introit, Collect, Gradual, Preface). The chances for recovering an understanding of this unity seem slight, for several reasons: the choice of language; the different world view of many of the propers; and the shift in emphasis from an otherworldly to a this-worldly cast in religion. To identify with thought forms which are no longer relevant is difficult, and therefore the simple translation of some parts of the worship service into modern English misses the point. If the underlying thrust or emphasis of the propers is not the emphasis of today, no amount of translation can overcome its remoteness. We cannot convert modern men into medieval men—nor should we try!

There is at the heart of most churches a small group of people for whom the liturgical system of the church is meaningful. They have taken the time to study it; they understand it; they have mentally manipulated it so that it continually relates to them; and they have experienced its great worth and deep richness. For a growing percentage of people, however, if worship is not immediately understandable it will never be understood. And there is no reason why this should not be so. Why should we make a central part of our Christian life, one which should be spontaneous and joyful, so difficult to understand? If we are serious about celebrating the presence of Christ, we should be serious about forms of worship that make such celebration possible.

There is another side to the whole problem. When worship is cast in language which is out of date, the implication is that worship as a whole is out of date. More seriously, the implication is that Christianity is the burden of the past and has no true contemporaneity. True, few people would be prepared to admit that this is the impression they want to give, but the important thing is that this is the impression others receive. Many people within the church and outside it have, over the last five years, expressed to me their dissatisfaction with the worship life of the congregation—and this feeling of outdatedness is a key reason! Those truly tuned in to the Christian way of life feel cheated when their worship with the community of Christ is not as contemporary as their personal faith; conversely, many people feel the worship life of the church so outmoded that they lose a concept of the practicality of worship. The church as a whole remains quite silent on the subject, despite much writing and experimentation, which may itself be an indication that we are no longer sure we are right in remaining with the "tried and true." There are many pastors today who confide that they receive nothing from the worship service they are called to conduct on Sunday mornings, and that their own spiritual needs are better serviced through small groups within the church, individual conversations with parishioners, or groups of like-minded clergy. If this is true of a growing number of ministers, why the reluctance to change?

Perhaps we are reluctant to change because we do not trust the Spirit to lead us into all truth, including the truth of a rejuvenated worship life. Perhaps we are reluctant to change because we have a concern for the united worship of a denominational tradition. Perhaps we are reluctant to change the liturgy because the church seems wary of changes in almost all aspects of its life. Perhaps we are reluctant to change the pattern of the worship life of the church for the simple reason that it is the most sensitive area—the area in which the greatest number of people are involved.

Whatever the reason for our reluctance, it is nonetheless true that part of the solution to the renewal of the church in our century lies in radical new approaches to meaningful worship. If Christ is risen and is the Head of his body, the church, the future lies open for new things under the Spirit of God. Among these new things we must count creative new worship.

Creativity is not limited to a few scattered individuals in the churches of the world. In American Lutheranism, for example, there is a proposed new rite of Holy Communion, authored by the Inter-Lutheran Commission on Worship, which will offer a creative new setting for the church as a whole.

The ILCW rite does several interesting things. For one, it moves the hymn, "Glory to God in the Highest" to the opening of the service and thus restores the element of praise at the very beginning of worship. The Creed is viewed in this service as a response to the total service of the word, and hence it follows not only the lessons but also the sermon. The Confession and Absolution are placed, in a new written form which is quite exciting and modern, ahead of the liturgy of the sacrament instead of at the beginning of worship. The Peace is extended through a handclasp, as has been common in contemporary forms of worship. The bread is broken as part of the action of the Eucharist to symbolize the brokenness of Christ for the world. The rubrics for the service encourage the use of laymen and additional ministers in the performance of the rite, which is also good, since it broadens the base of participation. The entire service has been translated into contemporary English and makes a pleasing setting for some liturgical innovation which does not veer too far from the traditional and yet captures the modern spirit. The ILCW rite is only one attempt among many, but it bears the legitimation of a larger, more representative group within the churches than do the individually-written contemporary services which are currently more common.

The time for individual communities of Christ to begin expressing themselves creatively in worship is upon us. No longer can we be satisfied with "edifying discourses" at worship; the existence of a meaningful sermon at the heart of the ordinary Protestant service is no longer (was it ever?) enough to save the total worship life of the church. It has too long resulted in the "cult of personality" for the preacher; besides, anyone can buy good books to read today on the subject of religion-in-general or Christianity-in-particular. Christian worship, however, can regain its meaning as it becomes the genuine possession of a *community* of Christ, rather than a spectator sport in which the participants are choir, clergy, and an occasional lector.

In order to create such new worship, the community as a whole must commit itself to the liturgical task. The job cannot, in the end, be carried off by an alert pastor or "layman" alone. What is needed is nothing less than the eventual creation of a total experience for that community, an experience in which the needs of the community are brought before God and God is brought before the needs of the community in this conversation we call worship. This may be partially achieved, from a technical viewpoint, through such a simple thing as the inclusion of periods of silence, so that the needs of individuals may be spoken into the heart of the community. The experience of East Harlem Protestant Parish, where the ministers first walk into the congregation to gather together the needs of the community and then spin pastoral prayers based on those needs, has been rewarding.

It is possible for community interpretation of the Bible, by means of a committee ranging from young to old and crosscutting economic, social, and racial divisions, to create a situation in which the preaching of the church really comes alive again. Such interpretation can truly speak to the needs of the total community.

The goal is the achievement and creation, over a long period of experimentation, of a style of worship which is indigenous to the community. Only in such a way will the blinding factors and excess baggage of so much of the church's worship life be surgically removed in order that liturgy can again breathe life. It is still possible to teach people the meaning of the current liturgies of the churches, but the question is, Why bother? If Christ is our eternal Contemporary, in our joy and sorrow, shouldn't the worship life of the church proclaim that contemporaneity?

There is one question left to answer before launching into a program of revamping the liturgy. What in the existing tradition of the church's worship life is meaningful? What is not? What should we retain, in however altered a form, in order to develop a pattern of worship which will have some link with the tradition? What can be cast off as so much excess and diversionary baggage?

Before we get to this, there are a few leftover preliminaries. For one thing, there must be a conviction on the part of the community—or at least a percentage of it—that liturgical experimentation is not a gimmick. If such contemporary worship patterns are gimmicks, then all worship is a gimmick. Who has established the lines of judgment that read: Anything new and original in worship is a gimmick; anything old and familiar is not? Why is it not possible to reverse the decision and conclude that the old thing is a gimmick whereas novelty and originality are the reality? After all, what is a gimmick but a tool of deception, whereby reality is hidden for a while? A gimmick is a trick, and tricks have no place in real life. The older patterns of worship may be tricks for those who can't possibly relate to them. Those who protest new worship forms as gimmicks have made three decisions: (a) only the old and traditional has value; (b) we have made our own judgment about the criteria of a worship experience; and (c) there is no need for worship to relate to life in a meaningful way. To these, we need to answer: Then the entire worship life of the church is automatically called into question, because truly to be worship it must relate to life!

Secondly, worship should be inclusive and not exclusive; it should not arbitrarily cut people off from an experience. It should not be built on such exclusive terms that "one from the outside world" is unable to get the message. The umbrella of Christ's resurrection, in other words, should cast its shade on all who are present, since it is part of the task of the church to celebrate the victory of the resurrection on behalf of the world and for the sake of all men. Certainly the inclusive love of the community is an essential factor in this process.

The final forms of a congregation's revitalized worship should not be so specific that they rule out the legitimate concerns of a portion of the congregation. This can only be demonstrated by example: if a congregation wants to hold a worship service centered on the theme of Air Pollution, it may be better to settle more generally on a theme such as The Care of the Earth, into which theme the community could fit concerns such as air and water pollution, industrial wastes, crowded skies, and environmental hazards. It might be objected that this will dull the cutting edge of contemporary worship. Against this, it must be said that the cutting edge of worship is broader than one specific

current event. For example, if Genesis 2 and the following chapters have something to say about the care of
the creation and man's dominion over nature, then that
something can be said for many situations, not just for
one. The specifics can be spelled out in the shape of the
prayers, the opening confession, the period of silence
for out-loud prayer by individuals, and the postcom-
munion liturgy. If any one of these concerns is adver-
tised as the single reason for this worship experience,
some members of the congregation will be arbitrarily
cut off from the experience.

But now to the specific question: What is meaningful? I have been involved in experiences not of my own
creation and in many of my own design, and I have
come to the conclusion that (especially for churches of
the liturgical tradition) there are four parts of traditional
worship which retain their meaning when cast into new
forms. These four parts are: a declaration of forgiveness; a liturgy of the word; an offertory; and a liturgy
of the Eucharist.

A DECLARATION OF FORGIVENESS

God is both remote from and near to man. His near-
ness is most clear in Christ, but Christ is still not the
whole story about God. We speak of Christ as a final
revelation of God, as a "window through which we
see God," and in other terms; yet God remains hidden
even within the figure of Christ. This hiddenness or remoteness of God is related to the Bible's concept of
"holiness." God is holy, that is, he is "totally other"
than man. He is related to man despite, not because of,
his difference from man. The uniqueness of the Christian proclamation lies in this, that God and man can

be united in fellowship with one another despite their difference. The link is the biblical truth that man is created "in the image of God"; this is the basis for our communication with God.

Our awareness of our difference from God has been called "awe"; it is the kind of feeling you get standing before a breathtaking natural wonder such as the Grand Canyon. It is the type of feeling men get in the presence of a fantastically beautiful woman. The limitations of man are sharply recognizable when we stand in this relationship to God, and our reflection on our limitations makes us acutely aware that we have not come near to doing the will of God in our lives; maybe we don't even know what God's will is! It has therefore been recognized that, in order for a meaningful communion with God to take place, there must be a "clearing of the boards with God." In Christianity, this takes place in the knowledge that God forgives man and enables him to begin anew to seek his will in each moment of life. This is the reason we speak of a "declaration of forgiveness" rather than of a "confession." The positive side of the ledger must be stressed; namely, that sin—man's separation from God, from the world, from other people, and from himself—is forgiven in and through the cross of Christ. Therefore, we do not dwell on the fact of sin, but move on into the healing light of God's love. We need to hear that God accepts us as we are in order that we can begin to accept others as they are.

I am convinced that one of the four main parts of a worship experience should be this "declaration of forgiveness." Beyond this, the whole shape of the confession and absolution in contemporary worship should be determined by the theme for the service as a whole. I have therefore written what might be called specific confessions in general form. For example, if the theme of the worship experience is, Freed by Christ to Serve Others, the confession and absolution might well be shaped to seek the love of God for the points in our lives where we have not (a) recognized our freedom, or (b) accepted it, or (c) exercised it. There will always be time in other experiences for the expression of failure in various areas of life; in order to shape a worship experience along one specific theme, however, the "declaration of forgiveness" may well set the tone.

Many people are unable to express their need for a new type of experience in worship. The fact remains that they have this need, and they often recognize it. Psychologists indicate that one of the great problems of modern man is a combination of a low self-image and a feeling of unresolved guilt. People need to receive a word of forgiveness for the areas in their lives where they cannot forgive themselves for failings, real or imagined. Imagined failings cannot, of course, be dealt with in liturgical forms; they require more help from professional psychology. But real failings can be dealt with if God's call to begin life anew each day is realistically sounded at the beginning of worship, in order that people can identify it as a word true for them.

Why shape specific confessions in "general" form? The general confession of sins in much of liturgical worship has lost its power. The reason for this is less likely to be the language involved than the fact that, where a general confession of sin is utilized week in and week out, people eventually dull their awareness of specific problems in their lives. The consequence is that, instead of confessing all their sins, they wind up confessing none of them—and therefore feel no release when the word of God's love is sounded. It simply does not relate to them in any meaningful way. Where specific forms are used, confession and absolution become meaningful. This portion of the service, then, a declaration of forgiveness, ought to be retained in a modern experience of worship because it has a great deal of meaning when reshaped.

It is quite possible to achieve an atmosphere of confession and absolution without going into a lot of specifics. In some experiences of worship, where people are open and real to each other, where the arena of trust and love is so evident that the spirit is contagious, there is little need to spell everything out. But usually help is needed, and that is why we choose in most instances to be very explicit.

At this point, permit a small tangent on the use of verbal communication in worship. Without verbal communication, I feel, worship has little chance of getting off the ground. Against this, of course, stands a clear tradition of silence in worship in the Quaker fellowship. But even here the silence is broken by words when someone feels the need to communicate with the group. What I have consciously tried to do with words in worship is to use them as tools toward an experience. To do this, they must be honest words. You cannot put words into someone else's mouth unless you are confident they will ring true for him. And you cannot expect them to ring true at all unless they first ring true in the pit of your own life. I believe that words which are honestly written can relate to other people. I have not given up on verbal communication; in fact, I believe a new day of verbal communication is about to dawn for many, many people. But honesty is absolutely essential. Anyone who cannot write an honest liturgy had better not try to write any liturgy at all.

Beyond the crucial first step of honesty, I also believe it necessary to use words as sharply as possible. We should try to raise the level of communication by the sharpness of our language. By this I certainly do not mean that our language should be coarse and harsh, but rather that it should be so pointed that it is virtually impossible for anyone to exclude himself from the circle of meaning. Anyone familiar with the Bible can sense that this is the way the great prophets of Israel, among many others, used language. Their words struck home, for better or for worse.

Within the rhythm of life we described in chapter 1, the opening portion of the service, a declaration of forgiveness, is approximately the same thing as *awareness*. Awareness consists in having the eyes opened to a need or a problem which must be solved in life. In the context of contemporary worship, when the opening confession and absolution are shaped into the theme of the worship as a whole, it serves in this capacity. The reason for a specific confession in general form thus becomes the sensitizing of the congregation to a particular need in life or to a particular problem with which they must grapple. They are made aware of this problem in the form of the confession; they are made aware of their need for God's assistance in coming to grips with it in confession and absolution. In order to serve as a means of developing awareness, the opening confession and absolution in my contemporary worship experiences have been, rather than abbreviated, lengthened into sev-

eral congregational responses which deal with the theme
for the evening. The release given in the absolution is a
release to confront the problem, however, not to aban-
don it. It is an experience of God's trust in us to deal
with the problem realistically and meaningfully.

A LITURGY OF THE WORD

The liturgy of the word is that portion of the service
in which we carry on a conversation with God based on
his word to us in Scripture and our response to him.
Within the churches of the liturgical tradition, many
hymns of praise and small anthems have been used
essentially as the setting in which to place the diamond
of God's word.

What is essential in a liturgy of the word? Many
people today have little understanding of the signifi-
cance of the Kyrie, the Gloria Patri, and the Gloria in
Excelsis. Rather than attempt to recapture their meaning through modern settings to these anthems, I have
been led into a stress on their place by substituting
modern hymns which give glory to God for his gifts
in Christ and secondarily in word and sacrament, whose
words are instantly recognizable as this glorification.
Such hymns set a tone of receptivity for the word of
God which, in many cases, is more effective than the
tone set by even modern settings to the ancient anthems
of praise. I would therefore suggest stripping these items
from the liturgy, not permanently, but for the sake of
achieving better understanding through this initial
substitution.

If this suggestion is followed, there remain five parts
of the liturgy of the word worthy of retention:

1. An entrance declaration (spoken/sung in unison).
2. A prayer.
3. Scripture readings from Old Testament, Epistle and Gospel; and, possibly, readings from contemporary authors whose words either challenge one to follow God's will or reflect a world view definable in Christian terms.
4. A response to the word, either in terms of a traditional creed or by a creed shaped by the liturgical committee of the church, preferably in hymn form.
5. A contemporary declaration of the word, preferably based on the Gospel for the day.

Let us examine each of these in turn.

Since it is no longer the custom of the clergy to enter the sanctuary at the beginning of the liturgy of the word, following the declaration of forgiveness, it might be worthwhile to consider stressing the entrance of the congregation as a whole into an attitude of conversation with God. If the Introit no longer seems to serve its original function, why not change the Introit to a congregational reading of entrance? Such an entrance declaration could be sharply structured in terms of the theme for the service as a whole and would lead people into thinking on the problem or need which underlies the service.

In connection with the prayer, I suggest a shift from normal procedure. This shift would be to place the prayer called the Collect in the context of prayers following the liturgy of the word. The reason for this is that the tone for the day has not yet been fully set. The Collect serves as a means of putting in prayer form petitions resulting from a consideration of the theme set for the service. The use of a Collect at this time thus seems premature. In place of the Collect you may want to use a short prayer for the right hearing of the word, a prayer urging people to separate God's word from man's and calling them to open themselves to God's word.

The Scripture lessons should be carefully chosen so that they relate to the theme for the day. The retention of Scripture lessons in such a unified form is not only desirable, it is virtually a necessity. The Protestant church has long said it lives out of the word of God, in dependence on God's word to man in Scripture. If we drop Scripture from our worship pattern, we will automatically minimize the importance of the Bible in our tradition. At the same time, we will destroy the very reason for having a liturgy of the word in the first place. The word speaks to man today. Some of the difficult lessons in many churches' readings seem to deny this. But Scripture does still speak to men, and the search should be made for passages which are quite easily understood by the congregation.

A word about the sermon: it has a place. If the church as community of Christ is the tool for the fulfillment of God's will, there will always be a place for the interpretation of that will. If the church as community of Christ is the place of celebration of the gospel, then there will always be a place for proclaiming that gospel. Much contemporary preaching suffers because it is neither a celebration of the gospel nor an interpretation of God's will, but a compilation of maxims and *bons mots* which strike the preacher's fancy. I am convinced, through experience, that no one is closed to a proclamation of the word. What people are closed to is a translation of the authority of the word into the authori-

tarianism of the preacher. The preacher can easily transform the pulpit into a totalitarian enterprise when he
loses sight of his commission as herald of the kingdom.
Young people are quick to sense this; they are equally
ready to hear an honest proclamation of the word with
no frills.

The impact of Jesus' teaching and preaching seems to
have been enhanced by its brevity, if the Gospels are
reliable at this point. There is a point of mystery in
much of the proclamation of Jesus; much is left to the
imagination of the hearer. The task of preaching in our
day seems better served by brevity than bravado, by
limitation than by loquaciousness, by open-endedness
rather than complete wrap-up. The listener has a responsibility when he hears a sermon. Too often he is
robbed of the exercise of his responsibility by having
all the answers given to him—especially the answers to
questions which he is not asking! Better ten or even
five minutes of tightly packed, sharply pointed, well-
interpreted Scripture, filtered through personal experience, and with an open-ended application than twenty-
five minutes of rambling moralism.

Within the rhythm of life set forth in chapter 1, the
liturgy of the word correlates to confrontation. In this
portion of the service, we enter into conversation with
God to find the tendencies he has revealed which help
in finding a solution to the problem. To confront a
problem means to seek understanding of its nature and,
simultaneously, seek different ways to solve it. But the
problem must really be yours, and the solution must
ultimately be yours. This is why we speak of God revealing tendencies to a solution and not ready answers.
The answers must be your own. In the setting of con-

temporary worship, the liturgy of the word serves as man's confrontation with the problem, based on some input from the will and desire of God. We have outlined a way to shape the liturgy of the word so that this confrontation can be quick, sharp, and to the point.

AN OFFERTORY

This is the most neglected and misunderstood aspect of the worship service. Many people see it as the time when they "fork over" money to keep the institution rolling another week. There is little connection between the envelope deposited in the offering basket on Sunday morning and the work of the church in service to community, home, and individual during the week. Similarly, there is little connection between the offering and the Eucharist which fulfills the service. One reason for this is the scarcity of Holy Communion in much Protestant worship. Despite the emphasis of the liturgical renewal on the full service of word and sacrament, despite the national statements of various denominations, Protestant worship as a whole is still characterized by a starvation diet when it comes to the Lord's Supper. This alone is enough cause for the divorce of offering and sacrament.

Yet we have listed the offertory as one of the four most important items in a worship pattern. In the face of so much misunderstanding, this seems almost ridiculous. But consider again the rhythm of life outlined in chapter 1. Where does the third point, commitment, fit into the worship service? If we look at the meaning of the offertory a moment, we can see that this correlates to that aspect of the rhythm of life we call commitment. The offertory is the sign of man's offering himself in service to God and world. It is, further, the offering of the world and its created products (symbolized by bread and wine) to the care of God. It forms the beginning of a pattern in which God sets apart that which is common for a divine purpose. This includes *us!* The conclusion, then, to the problem we have confronted in the liturgy of the word is found in the offertory, where we are challenged to enter into service of God's will in solution of the problem, and where, on the other hand, God demonstrates his loving presence. The offering prayer should then be specifically shaped to point to an offering of gifts, of manufactured products, of the world, and of the individual Christian in service to the solution of the problem under discussion. In this sense, *offertory* means "commitment."

Offertory means that the solution to the problem, not altogether cleared up, must come from us—working out of the framework of the love/trust community and in the knowledge of our acceptance by God. Offertory means that the challenge has been accepted and wrestled with, and that we know we are capable of dealing with the problem. From this viewpoint, the offertory has overtones of what is often called "mission": knowing that God has laid on us the responsibility for handling the situation and that he trusts us to do it, what alternative have we, if we are honest to God—and to ourselves—but to go out and get the show on the road?

There is some pretty meaningful stuff happening in the offertory, when you consider it this way. At this point in contemporary worship services, we have experienced a real drive "into the world," knowing that we can trust ourselves to deal with the problem because both the community and God trust us to deal with it.

We have already confronted the problem in worship; we have come to some conclusions about its solution; we are now ready to go out.

A suggestion: there must be some true links forged among offering, community, and Eucharist. For this reason, an offertory procession can be meaningful. When a little background information on this is given, the offertory procession can be one of the most meaningful parts of the service. By this we mean that the bread and the wine for the Eucharist come out of the midst of the community; the money received is brought up with the bread and wine, symbolizing the giving of a portion of ourselves. Usually, I ask someone to bring the bread and wine for the service and to consider that their offering (materially speaking).

The offertory prayers should then be carefully pointed so that no one can escape the call to offer himself as a whole person in the solving of the problem under consideration. At this point, we risk the judgment that he who refuses to offer himself is truly unworthy of sitting at the table of the Lord in communion, since he is not involved anymore. Since he has refused to risk himself in the solution to the problem, there can be nothing for him to celebrate at this point. The offertory, in the cycle of worship, is the crucial final step before the fulfillment of the community in celebration of the Lord's Supper. Without it, celebration is meaningless.

A LITURGY OF THE EUCHARIST

The liturgy of Holy Communion itself correlates to "celebration" in the rhythm of life outlined in chapter 1. The Lord's Supper is the point in the service which concretely demonstrates the deep communion which exists between man and his brother man and between mankind and God, and the harmony between mankind and the creation. It is the point of the celebration of life, but—and this is very important—not life fragmented and broken, but life whole, which is to say life *in* Christ *under* God *with* mankind and *properly related to* nature. This is what makes the Eucharist a Christian celebration!

The Eucharist is the most human of all the portions of the service; the key to it is the relationships God has created between man and fellowman through Christ. Too long has the church put down the human community by exaggerating the divine-human communion in the sacrament. There is a balance here we ought to strive to retain. By the same token, to view the Eucharist as solely a celebration of brotherhood will also miss the point; God is deeply involved here as well as man. Perhaps this diagram will help us understand:

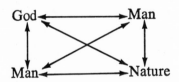

This diagram is an oversimplified picture of life as God intends it to be. We can experience it to be true. If we would draw that line beginning to the left of the diagram through "God—man," we must automatically extend the line through the whole diagram. When man's relationship with God is destroyed, in other words, his relationship with his fellowman is also destroyed and his harmony with and proper dominion over nature is ultimately destroyed. This is the situation of man under

God—before Christ. Christ, however, whom Paul called "the Second Adam," unblocked the passages once again in such a way that man may now experience through him life as it was meant to be. Holy Communion is the point in the worship service of the church where this should be evident!

In order to unblock some of the paths to this deep meaning of Holy Communion, we need to reevaluate this portion of the service. When we do, we find we should place more emphasis on the "sharing of the peace" than is customary. In my experience it has been best to reinstitute the peace through the passing of a handclasp through the congregation, beginning from the minister. With some meaningful words about the message of the peace as background, this can be a moving experience. It can be the recognition of the interrelationship of God-man-fellowman-nature, as indicated by our diagram.

The distribution of Holy Communion is best done with plain materials. Bread and wine are common gifts of both the earth and the manufacturing processes of man. They bear a good meaning today. Some have suggested Coke and pretzels, others coffee and doughnuts; while I would have no real objection to this, I feel content using the materials Christ used for the sacramental observance. The bread should be leavened; if it cannot be baked by someone in the congregation who then considers it her offering, it should be bought fresh the day of the service to serve as a reminder of its earthiness and its manufactured state. We are offering here not the creation, but the creation bent through us— with all the faults and problems and joys of labor poured into it at the same time. This may sound like heavy symbolism, but it is readily recognizable in the context of the service.

To celebrate the unity of man with his fellowman, you may want to move in the direction of having each person receive his bit of bread and sip of wine from the person next to him; he, in turn, passes it on with the words, "Jim (or Sally or Tom), the body of Christ, broken for you . . . Jim, the blood of Christ, shed for you." In a congregation where the parishioners know each other, this makes an especially meaningful addition to the regular Communion service.

The Holy Communion should be the most joyful part of the service; it should be the point at which spontaneous joy breaks forth in the atmosphere of love and concern that is built up throughout worship. Holy Communion is, therefore, closely related to everything that precedes it. It comes as a true fulfillment of the worship service.

But what of the situation beyond this? All that can be said is that Holy Communion should be the "fuel" that propels us into the world to do God's work there. If Communion shuts off at the dismissal (or benediction), then it is being walled in by the church and not being shared with the world. The reason (in older liturgies) for the speedy end to worship after Communion is directly related to this. Rather than sit and dwell on the meaning of Communion within our cloistered walls, we are deliberately forced out into the world, where the message of the gospel and the relevance of the sacraments must be as real as they are within the narrow confines of a worship experience. It seems best that the closing portion of the service. following the distribution of Communion, should be deliberately shaped to

propel people into the world, still—as it were—"munch-
ing on the concerns" of the service. If this means that
worship is inconclusive, that's exactly what it should
mean! It is time to show clearly that the end of worship
really is the beginning of service; worship is a "slice of
life" experience. The conclusion to the service ought to
be shaped to show this.

Although all of these points have not been discussed
in detail, it can be seen that the truly important elements in the liturgy of the Eucharist are the following:

1. Sharing the peace—"showing our community"
2. The eucharistic prayer—"the pastor's bailiwick;
    done by him for the people"
3. The Lord's Prayer—"the table grace of the people
    of God"
4. The distribution—"establishing contact"
5. The send-off—"back to the world, people!"

Around these can be built an exciting celebration!

These are the parts of the liturgy I find meaningful.
They have become meaningful through a lot of work. It
is an uphill battle to find out what portions of the traditional liturgy really relate to people today. You too
must make the journey.

What we are talking about here is the abandonment
of a sense of obligation in worship in favor of the development of a worship experience which will automatically and spontaneously appeal to a broad cross section
of people. Those who feel obligated to "go to church,"
as if some outside force were pushing them there (a
force they sense is not God) will have difficulty. Those
who attend because they sense that after all something is
happening in worship are tuned in. It may take a lot of
failures; this is, in the end, unimportant. What is im-

portant is to make the honest attempt to let worship break out where it can!

The aim of liturgical innovation should be the development of a total Christian environment. We see four characteristics in such an environment. The first characteristic is *love*. When worship is truly taking place, a sense of love permeates the atmosphere. In this sense, the worship life of the church is a safe harbor for the Christian. It is the place where his masks can all fall down and he can be released from the boxes the world would put him in; a place where he can be himself and be accepted as such, because God has accepted him in Christ. It is the place where the butterfly that is "I" is given new birth in the chrysalis that is "We."

If we Christians believe that all love comes finally from God, then worship (in a broad sense) occurs wherever true love is found. In a worship service, we are homing in on a feeling of love which is not exclusive but inclusive; it is a love which does not rule anyone out of its circle but rather includes all in that circle. Love is the foundation stone of the total environment of worship, and it is remarkably spontaneous. It can be felt!

The second characteristic is corollary to the first. It is *trust*. Without deep love, trust cannot happen. Without deep trust, love cannot happen. When we sense an atmosphere of trust, in which each person relates to his brother as he is, then trust is happening. In the end, you cannot really learn to trust anyone. Intellectual pointers toward a situation of trust can be given, but they alone cannot bring someone to a condition of trust. Trust can only be felt and reacted to in concert with other people. The trust you feel coming from other people will, in turn, make you a more trusting person toward others . . .

and so the circle grows wider. Trust is one of the key aspects of a total environment of worship. It is difficult within the current forms to express it; new forms are needed, in order that trust may be demonstrated within the context of worship.

The third characteristic is *concern*. This concern can show itself in two ways. First, there is a concern shared by the entire community, which is pointed out into the world. In this sense, concern merges into what has been called the "mission" of the church. It is important that the concerns of the community be built up in worship; if they are not, the extension of worship into the world is aborted. Worship cannot operate in a vacuum. This is what so many young people sense as one of the critical problems in much of the church's worship. "Church" is a safe harbor and, apparently, nothing more—for a large number of people. Where concerns have been sharply delineated and honestly confronted, and some conclusions have been drawn about the direction life ought to take, there worship no longer operates in a vacuum but is the true point of dispersion of the community into the world. Here is where Jesus' sayings about the leaven in the lump, the city set on the hill, the salt of the earth, begin to make sense.

On the other hand, concern for each other must mark the worship environment of the church. This is again a barrier to many people seeking an experience of worship. They want and need people to be concerned with them, with their weaknesses and their strengths, and yet so often they see the level of concern never rising above trivialities. In order to develop a concern for someone else, you must have a genuine love for that person; along with that goes trust in him as a person. Many people are turned away at the first step in the procedure. They can never feel the love for themselves as persons, which should be evident, when petty concerns fill the air. When the worship experience is to the point, and when it gives persons the opportunity to speak freely into the community, true concern can be felt again. The two polarities of concern, then, the concern for the individual and the concern of the community for the world, must be part of the total environment of worship.

The fourth characteristic of a total environment of worship is *honesty,* both intellectual and emotional. We must be able to "come clean" in the presence of our brothers. Part of the mask that many people wear is an intellectual mask. They hide their true feelings under a veneer of knowledge; conversely, there are those who hide their true knowledge under a veneer of feeling. But man is not really divided like this; he is all of a piece. When the raw edges of what a man believes deep within himself, both emotionally and intellectually, are felt in the verbal portions of worship, he will be heard; and people will drop their masks in his presence. What he says may be rejected, but he will be respected as a person, for his honesty. And so it works for everyone in the midst of a worship experience.

Two last things must be said. I believe it is possible to develop a total environment on the basis of the foregoing outline of the things I feel are important. There has been no intention to rule out the use of modern mass communications techniques in worship patterns, although they have not been mentioned. If they can be used honestly, fine. Just ask: Will it have meaning? Will it help develop the pattern? Or will it be a gimmick?

Each man must find his own way in dealing with such matters. I have laid out a bald outline for developing a meaningful worship experience. The criterion to use when deciding about the possible use of additional material is, whether the use of this thing adds to or detracts from the total environment of love, trust, concern, and intellectual and emotional honesty.

The final word is this. The planning cannot be done by one individual. Coming through the back door, we have stumbled onto the idea that Christian worship is essentially corporate, is communal in nature. God is found in community because God is personal, which finally means that God's love is experienced through persons and other means outside ourselves. Remember, baptism is not baptism without people; the Lord's Supper is not a supper without the guests; and even preaching is not preaching except for the active listeners of the community. The experience of God's love, trust, concern, and honesty toward man comes in the shape of a community of individuals who, because they know themselves accepted by God through Christ, can in turn mediate God-in-Christ to others. Here I have come to the ragged edge of describing the community of Christ as a "sacramental people." These "sacramental people" are the signs of God's presence in the world; they are the "material" through which the "spiritual" comes to others. Imperfect they certainly are! Frequently unloving, and griping about lots of things. But in the total environment of worship they are tuning in to each other as they are tuning in to God, and in turn they can tune in to the world. It's a beautiful thing to experience.

3

Putting Your
Thing Together

Let's put all this into your parish. What do you need to be able to enter into contemporary worship patterns? What is the minimum number of raw materials you can begin with? What are some of the technical pitfalls to avoid?

The first two chapters dealt with understanding worship. Now we must explore further, and deal with the technical side of developing meaningful worship. Not that following the lines laid down here will guarantee a good worship experience. But it will help you to avoid technical difficulties that can stand in the way of that good experience; it will help you to tear down some of the barriers to worship.

The first practical need should be obvious. You must have people interested in helping to create contemporary worship patterns and people who will help in the technical work of putting a service together. The latter should be easy to find. The former may not be easy to find, because most people are unaccustomed to working out either their own or congregational worship patterns. To begin, it is enough if you can gather a small core of interested people who will work to put the thing together on a practical level. Then the basic work can be done by the pastor or the board of worship or a handful of creative people. I believe that, given enough time and experience, the dikes will burst and the creative work will become communal.

It is necessary to prepare the congregation for new worship, if you seek to avoid misunderstanding. This can be done by showing materials and explaining them to the committee on worship in your parish, getting them excited about something different and new. It may take surprisingly little effort on your part for people to become open to the idea of a new form of worship service.

One cautious church went through the process of contacting churches holding contemporary worship services on a regular basis to find out the reaction of the congregations. Only then did they enter into such a program. Though this may seem to be too much work, it could pay off in the long run where there is a lot of hesitancy or misunderstanding.

The church paper or newsletter can be used to explain the purpose and nature of contemporary worship over a period of several weeks or months. For a six-month period the pastor of one church devoted his columns in the newsletter to an explanation of worship; then the congregation participated in the first of an eventual series of contemporary services.

When the preparatory work is done and a small group of people has been gathered to put the experience together, the next obvious need is for leaders in music. It may sound surprising, but you don't need to have a large group of musicians in order to create a worship experience. Many small churches hesitate because they feel they don't have the resources in this area. While it may be desirable to have a large group, you really only need someone who can lead in singing. An *a cappella* service may not sound exciting to you now, but it can be as edifying as one in which a large choir and many musicians or a magnificent organ play a prominent role.

It may be hard to believe, but contemporary worship patterns will strike instant chords in the hearts of a broad cross section of a congregation (even where it is feared they will not). Contemporary worship appeals to people from literally seven to seventy-seven, for various reasons: the freshness of the service, a sincere interest in the people (very likely, young people) who put the worship service together, and the exhilaration of participating in a worship experience that has been carefully worked out. You may hear such comments as: "I've never fully realized the meaning of Holy Communion until this service"; or "This was the most meaningful worship service I've ever participated in."

A word of warning: do not expect that such forms of worship will appeal to everyone in the congregation, no matter how inclusive you have tried to make the service. There is always a percentage of people in the congregation whose link with the traditional church service gives them a security which they lack in other areas of life. With change going on all about them, they resist change in the worship of the church because it means, in their minds, that all of life is without a unifying center. Too, there may be a small percentage of people whose dislike for contemporary worship is rooted in their misconception of or hidden rejection of the gospel, which manifests itself when they are subjected to a worship service that truly relates to them. Finally, there are those who truly understand and appreciate older patterns of worship and for this reason find fulfillment in the status quo! And, of course, apathy is an overriding problem. No matter what you do, you can't please everybody. You simply have to try, and live with the results in hope.

One last thing that might be useful in preparing the congregation is to indicate (if it is true) that such experiences of worship are not meant to supplant the "normal pattern of worship on Sunday," but are meant rather to help people experience all worship anew. I have on occasion emphasized this and have found that it helps more people to see the point than otherwise would. People usually find it too threatening to consider such worship as the norm; that point of controversy is given a safety valve when contemporary services are viewed as aids to Sunday worship. Unfortunately, it is also often true that for a percentage of people (usually teens), especially in a large congregation, the contemporary services represent the only legitimate periods of worship. I would be less than candid if I did not stress that my desire is now for an eventual explosion of new forms of worship as the normal pattern of twentieth century worship.

The key to a good experience is to be found in three areas. The building of a sense of expectation is one area; this is done through some background education by means of personal presentation and printed material. The second is the small core of dedicated people who will put the service together and for whom this is a real service both to themselves and to the church at large. The third area is that of actual preparation, which is what the remainder of this chapter will explore.

RESOURCES

The congregation should be prepared to underwrite the expense of gathering enough musical materials to work out a hymnody for contemporary worship. A list of what we consider the best resources is found in the "Second Addition" to this book. Resources are essential. No congregation can enter into the creation of contemporary worship, complete with music, totally without help. Even though the eventual goal is the development of a worship form which reflects the needs and wants of a community of Christ, outside resources will always be necessary.

Enough materials (anthems, etc.) should be purchased at the outset for use by all members of a choir. The purchase of several quires of musical staff mimeograph stencils is a must, for you to be able to duplicate hymns for congregational use. You can build a library of cut stencils to be used again for future services. Since each musical staff stencil covers an entire page, nothing else can be written on it and its use is thus flexible in future programs. Check on copyright and reproduction rights and secure necessary permissions. Then, if credits are clearly listed, there should be no objections.

As part of your resources you should certainly count a file of contemporary worship services created by other congregations. A bulging file of outside material will enable you to put worship services together in various ways, and will offer the fruits of the work of others, which may be adapted for use in your local context. The development of such a file should be easy, since there is rarely a congregation anymore which is unaware of at least one other church which is experimenting in its worship life.

Tapes and records of modern music can also be helpful as resources. They will give you the tempo of contemporary hymns, which is frequently difficult to catch from printed music.

THE CHOIR

In my experience, it has been best to gather an *ad hoc* choir for contemporary worship. The choir should be gathered not so much on the ability of individuals to sing with professional tone, but rather on their commitment to and excitement about new forms of worship. If there is no junior choir in your congregation, here is one way to begin one. The group should consist of enough voices to lead in song, since this is a primary function of a choir. The size of the choir would therefore vary with the size of the congregation. In a small church you can get by with as few as four. (Indeed, even fewer: one of the most creative and exhilarating worship services I have ever experienced took place in a small church with one guitarist and one male soloist who led the singing.) For a large church, the number should begin around twelve for the sake of volume. Generally, the larger the choir, of course, the more flexible its use. I have seen choirs sing as many as three selections during worship apart from their use as song leaders.

With regard to dress, experience indicates that the choir feels more comfortable and is just as well accepted if the members are not vested for such a worship service. Ordinary clothes help to create an atmosphere of informality and spontaneity which is one of the keys to a good experience. Generally our choirs do not pack the stalls, either, but stand in front of the chancel.

If the congregation has a director of music, so much the better. If it is his job to direct the choirs of the church, the direction of choirs for contemporary worship should certainly be considered part of his job description. I am particularly indebted to an organist-choirmaster whose feeling for the meaningful in worship extends to a commitment to the contemporary worship choirs of the church.

In the case of a small congregation which has part-time organists, the pastor or the most interested individual should familiarize himself or herself with the music to be used, through records or tapes of other contemporary worship services. There is so much now available in records that, without any real musical knowledge, a small group could develop a large repertoire of hymns simply by studying the recordings and learning the chords for guitars given in most songbooks in this category.

The choir should be trained in the meaning and pattern of the worship of the church so that an understanding is built as to why certain things are done at certain times and why certain elements of worship are retained as meaningful. Of course, the choir should know in advance exactly what the particular service is about, how it is constructed, and what the congregation must do. Their leadership in this area helps to relax the congregation, which is often as hesitant and nervous as the choir during the first experience, and will likely continue to be so even in later experiences.

It is difficult to say how long one should practice with a choir for contemporary worship services. After a repertoire has been built up, things naturally become easier. For the beginning experiences, however, we would suggest three or four practice sessions, so that the music is very familiar and the choir can feel rather easy in its singing. Halfhearted attempts with a gigantic choir will fall flat; exuberant attempts by a cluster of people committed to the service and familiar with the music will succeed. Enthusiasm is catching!

THE DISTRIBUTION OF THE PARTS OF WORSHIP

In the early church, the key liturgical tasks of the pastor were the sermon and the eucharistic prayer. In liturgical churches today, this would have to be expanded to include the declaration of forgiveness. Worship is the proper work of the community, and for this reason we suggest that *everything possible should be handled by the people.* Select readers for all the lessons; they can be enlisted to find the lessons in contemporary writings most fitting for the service, also. Others can lead in the prayers. The choir should know its task, and should function without prompting. Let the musicians be led by one of their own. Anything which can possibly be handled by the people of a congregation should be given them as their responsibility in contemporary worship.

If it is the custom of the congregation to maintain a staff of ushers who are all adults, enlist and train young people for this task. If lighting effects and sound systems are available, make someone responsible for their use. Obtain the elements of Holy Communion through the girls or women of the church (more on this later).

In general, the rule of thumb to follow is that as much as possible be done by someone other than the pastor. The use of a large number of people in the actual conduct of a worship experience helps restore the sense of community which the early church understood and appreciated so much in its worship, and which is to a large extent lacking in our Sunday services. Again, this is not a gimmick but a real recovery of the community's responsibility for its worship life. If at all possible, let the pastor be responsible only for the sermon, the eucharistic prayer, and the declaration of forgiveness at the conclusion of the opening portion of worship.

THE MUSICIANS

A prior question must be dealt with before we speak about the musicians. What kind of worship service most encourages congregational participation? I have experienced jazz masses and have heard numerous efforts at rock-and-roll masses, but am convinced that the folk song form offers the best opportunity for total participation. The jazz mass form is useful for an occasional worship service and in congregations (of which there are a few) which have devoted a long time to "tuning in." The unfortunate thing, though, is that—with rare exceptions—the jazz mass form is something *done for* an audience, not something *entered into* by a congregation. The same is true of rock-and-roll masses, which have a value for young people and others who appreciate rock-and-roll, but most of which do not lend themselves easily to participation. The exception to this rule is in the case of using, as a hymn, a rock-and-roll song which is currently or recently popular (on this see below under "the use of secular materials"). For the deepest level of participation, however, the blend of folk song hymns and folk tunes to which hymn lyrics have been written is hard to beat. Such songs are most easily picked up by the congregation, and there are some which have already become classics in this field, such as "Sons of God" by James Theim or "They'll Know We Are Christians," by Peter Scholtes. Jazz and rock-and-roll masses have their place in a total round of liturgical patterns, but now, at least, they do not seem to be the fare on which the people of God can regularly feed and live.

Now, the musicians themselves. If a service is planned using folk forms, the best combination is a small combo made up of one lead guitarist, one rhythm guitarist, one banjo player, an acoustical bass player, with the possible addition of such extras as tambourine and drums. Barring this possibility (and it would be a rare congregation that could come up with all this at first), the musical group should be made up of as many guitarists as are available and want to do this sort of thing. There should, in addition, be some percussion instrument to carry a steady beat to support the choir and the congregation. Electric keyboards might also be used to carry the melody line. It is not necessary that the musicians be accomplished, although most young people who play the guitar know how to play it well or are working at it. The basic line of music is carried by the guitars; the players may be satisfied with chords rather than melody lines. The addition of an electric guitar is desirable, especially if you get into some of the hymns which lend themselves to harmonizing on an instrument. The hymn "What Will I Do?" by the Bawbees, for example, is a blues pattern and can be interspersed with rides on guitar and drums to build a total sound.

It is not advisable to use the church organ for such contemporary worship services, since the instrument does not lend itself readily to such music. Some forms of brass, if available, will add to the sound. As mentioned above, no musicians are absolutely essential, but a couple of guitars are desirable as the basic musical accompaniment.

It is best for the choir and the musicians to rehearse together and not separately, since they represent the total package of musical leadership for the congregation. They can better coordinate if they learn and work together.

One of the musicians should be designated as leader for the group, in order to coordinate their efforts. The musicians, as well as the choir, can function best as a group if they gather in front of the chancel. Their presence there is a stimulus to spontaneity and easiness for the congregation.

THE USE OF SECULAR MATERIALS

In medieval times, a lot of church music came off the streets. The lyrics of the songs were simply changed, and the tunes remained the same. So, for example, the song "Greensleeves" with altered lyrics became the traditional carol "What Child Is This?" This pattern is followed today by using common folk tunes with new lyrics that are religious in nature.

But the question beyond this is, What sort of materials can simply be taken lock, stock, and barrel from song charts for use in contemporary worship services? The criteria to follow here would depend on the individual, of course, but it is my feeling that songs relating to peace, justice, freedom, poverty, and other issues of the day are certainly acceptable within a worship experience. In general, songs that carry a message which is socially relevant or relevant in interpersonal relations may be used with good effect. Examples might include, in the category of the church's response to war, "The Great Mandella," by Peter, Paul, and Mary; "The Big Muddy," by Pete Seeger; "Blowin' in the Wind," by Bob Dylan; the old classic, "Where Have All the Flowers Gone?" and others. The problem of the individual in society is dealt with in such songs as "Eleanor Rigby," by the Beatles (a classic study of loneliness); and "Little Boxes," by Pete Seeger. A good song to emphasize the need for brotherhood might be "Get Together," by Dino Valenti, recorded by the Youngbloods. Freedom is hit hard in Tim Hardin's "Simple Song of Freedom." Much of the current underground music is usable in worship experiences. Since popular music shifts daily, however, the only way to keep up (if you do not listen to top-forty or underground stations on the radio) is through subscribing to one of the mass media newsletters, such as the *Bigler Report,* available through the Pittsburgh Council of Churches.

Readings abound in "secular" poetry and prose. Poets such as e. e. cummings, W. H. Auden, T. S. Eliot, Robert Frost, Carl Sandburg, Rod McKuen, and Leonard Cohen may be especially useful, along with numerous prose writers. Such readings may be used in addition to the Scripture for the service, under the heading "God speaks to us in the writings of today."

The church has long said that God reveals himself in contemporary poets and prophets; it must act on this belief. It must utilize materials from outside its walls to let God speak in as many forms as possible. Anyone with an ear to the radio can hear such poets at work all day long in the music of the young people. The use of such music can be varied. It can be used as an anthem, sung by the choir, in a service; or it can be simply used as an additional hymn from a "secular" source.

PUTTING THE PROGRAM TOGETHER

It is desirable to design a printed program that will be explicit. As long as you can keep everyone aware of what's happening in an unfamiliar setting, they will be at ease. Once they get lost, the service begins to lose its spontaneity and everyone gets worried about what's happening. This situation can be avoided if the printed program is well designed and executed.

The music for the program should be written out in full on musical staff stencils and reproduced. It may then be fit in at the right spot in the written program. Since it is not always possible to coordinate placement due to a break in writing over two pages, the best thing to do is indicate in the program itself exactly where the hymns (words and music) are found. Keep the hymns as close as possible to their placement in the service; one of my worst experiences came when the program and the music were printed separately and then slapped together. The congregation had to jump back and forth too much. The exception to the rule of music printed out would be those hymns set to folk tunes which are so familiar that no music is necessary. In this case, they can simply be printed in the bulk of the program.

Directions for the congregation should be printed in the program, either in italics or in parentheses. In that way, they are set off, yet attention is drawn to them as an important part of the service. Where there is a need to explain parts of the service orally, even this should be indicated so that people are not bothered when directions are given by the pastor or one of the leaders. The more precise and explicit you can get with your congregational directives, the easier the flow of the service. Why have people stumble on simple things?

All congregational responses should be written out, even if you feel that knowledge of them can be taken for granted. In a foreign setting, the most familiar things are easily lost. The service should be printed out in the fullest form possible.

The program may be printed on both sides of 8½-by-11 inch mimeo stock, since this is the size of the musical staff stencils. Colors might be used, but they should not be so dark as to obscure the printing in a dimly lit church. The use of different-colored paper throughout the program makes for a neat production.

Leave some space within the program or add a cover so that young people of the church can decorate it with art work. A note of warning here is that, unless there is a great deal of time, it should be simple art work so that it can either be transferred to stencils or done originally on them. A sad experience with linoleum block prints that did not dry in time taught me a lesson! As the congregation tore each page from the next one, the planners realized that we'd needed more time! If there is a lot of time available, this is fine. But where a regular program of contemporary worship is adopted it is probably impossible to do much more than stencil art work unless you have a large staff of artists on hand.

Whatever pattern of worship is followed for the service, it is helpful to indicate the parts of the service itself in print. (See the examples of folk masses in the "First Addition" below.)

The purpose of a program is to lead people beyond the level of technicalities into a framework that can enable a truly spontaneous worship experience. It may sound laborious to spend so much time on a printed program, but the effort pays off in the long run as people become more at ease and more able to participate fully in the service. I have known people who have said they couldn't get into a worship experience because they were so put off by a badly printed or badly put-together program that they got stuck at that level. Needless to say, it may have been their fault that they couldn't get involved; but why not develop a good printed program to eliminate this stumbling block once and for all?

ADDITIONAL MATERIALS

If the church lends itself to such usage, slides may be flashed on the chancel walls during the singing of hymns. This will create a total experience that can be quite interesting. It may, however, be a gimmick. Masscomm methods like this may be useful within a worship experience, but the information overload of the world as a whole might better be left at the church doorsteps. If the slide show lends meaning to the service, fine. But, if we work it right, words might come to have meaning again in the church, too!

A reminder at this point of something said before: the materials for the celebration of Holy Communion ought to be earthy. If possible, they should be prepared by members of the church. At least the bread could be home-baked. Those involved in preparing or obtaining the materials for the service should consider this their offering for the service itself. They are, in all likelihood, making a more thoughtful, if not more expensive, offering than most of the congregation.

And, again, the revival of an offertory procession in which the elements for communion are brought out of the midst of the congregation is also a highly effective symbol of the concept of offering. It says to the congregation that the work of our hands is worthy of consideration by God, and that it can be more of an offering of self than can coin.

Give careful thought to the traffic flow during the distribution of the elements. You eventually have to choose the best way to do this. Several ways are possible:

A. Table Communion at which the participants receive the broken loaf and themselves pass it down the Communion rail.

B. Passing the loaf out into the midst of the congregation.

C. Having a single file come past a freestanding altar to receive the elements of Communion.

D. If individual cups are necessary, why not use ordinary paper cups instead of the regular Communion ware? The commonness of the vessel serves to enhance the meaning of the sacrament in this case, in opposition to the long-standing thinking of the church. The change can help people think again about the meaning of Communion, and experience it anew.

E. The common cup is preferable for a folk mass because it helps to continue the concept of unity in Christ; as a matter of fact, a common mug or cup may be exactly the thing to emphasize the nature of the meal to the congregation.

Don't forget that there will be numbers of people beyond your own congregation who will be interested in this type of worship experience. Advertise at least the first one in order to get wide participation. If the first experience is successful, you may find that all succeeding efforts will advertise themselves, particularly if they are held on a regular basis.

Include the elements of worship *you* feel are essential. Follow your own integrity. If you simply want to rewrite Sunday morning's service, by all means do it. But become aware of the possibilities offered by other traditions, too. (Check chapter 2 again as to essentials of a worship experience.)

SHAPING THE EXPERIENCE

It is my belief, as spelled out in chapter 2, that each worship experience should be deliberately carved anew, even if you use the bones of the traditional service as the foundation on which to build. With the exception of simple rewrites of portions of Sunday services (which I followed in previous pastorates), when you are plunging into the waters of liturgical renewal, you might as well go to the deep end. Each contemporary worship experience in my recent history has been brand new. Certainly the bones are the same, but the flesh is different in each case. A lot of work is involved; let's not fool ourselves about that! But it can be tremendously rewarding and exciting for the people concerned. Here is where a real community decision can be made: What will be the theme of each worship experience? Once a

theme has been decided upon, you can pick it up and
run with it.

Again, choose themes that are inclusive and not exclusive. In other words, choose a theme that will include
as many concerns in a given area as possible. To pull
one aspect of a life-problem out of context as the theme
for an entire service means you are not willing to include the concerns of a lot of other people; ultimately,
it means that the service will relate to fewer and fewer
people—and that's not good. So pick a broad theme
and dump many areas of concern into it in the written
prayers, etc.

THE EUCHARISTIC PRAYER

The eucharistic prayer is such an important feature
of the service that it demands a few separate words. In
some churches, the custom reigns of using only the
words by which Christ instituted the sacrament as the
consecration. A growing number of churches, however,
are finding the use of a eucharistic prayer—that is, a
prayer spun around the words of institution—rewarding. Many good eucharistic prayers are in existence,
but here again the pastor really ought to try writing his
own, keeping in mind the theme of the service. The
eucharistic prayer is the pastor's domain, and it can be
extremely meaningful when it links the communion
with the life-problem that is the basis for the entire
service.

Eucharistic prayers are composed of at least three
basic elements:

A. An opening thanksgiving—a hymn of praise to God
   for his love for us in creation, in Christ, and in
   church. Some prayers rehearse a list of saints who

have special meaning in the life of the church because of their example of faith.

B. A remembrance of the life, death, and resurrection
of Christ with special emphasis on the meaning
of these events for our lives. In some eucharistic
prayers, the rehearsal includes a call to seek the
coming Presence of Christ. This section also includes, in most prayers, the words of institution.

C. A call for the Spirit of God to be present with the
congregation, drawing it together in love under
Christ, and asking for the blessing of the Spirit on
the bread and the wine of the sacrament. This is
then rounded out with an appeal for a worthy communion by the people, and some closing thanksgiving.

Eucharistic prayers can be shaped around these three
points, and they can be shaped in such a way as to
relate to the theme of the worship service as a whole.
They can have especially significant meaning when this
is done, for then we are tying our concerns to the sacrament which Christ instituted for our use; we are saying
that nothing can escape his blessing and that we are
capable of giving thanks to God for even the problems
of life we are called on to face as Christians. In the
"First Addition" to this book there are two examples of
eucharistic prayers that have been shaped to relate to
specific questions of life.

FINAL HELPS TOWARD SPONTANEITY

Don't worry about numbers. Worship experiences
neither succeed nor fail on the basis of the numbers of
people involved. It is important to have a commitment
to quality, not to quantity. Quality can come off with

four hundred people; it can come off with forty. Numbers play no factor in the development of the experience of worship, unless the number involved takes away from the spontaneity of the worship. Then and only then do numbers count.

We have taken recently to elongating our services through the inclusion of introductory materials such as a few poems and a short rehearsal of the congregation. The Scandinavian churches used to have a leader they called the *Klokker* who knew the music and helped the people to sing it. Our congregation has found the use of a "klokker" helpful toward breaking into spontaneity within the worship form.

It has often been thought that formal worship inhibits spontaneity. This is an unfair judgment. The point to remember is that if the form really relates to life then spontaneity will break out within the form.

One last help toward spontaneity in worship: occasionally use a setting other than the church building. Use other facilities which are available to hold the worship service. In our case, the coffee house at the church seems to provide a good atmosphere for a worship experience. In the church building, use a freestanding altar if possible.

Above all, don't be overly concerned about the technical aspects. Know what you're going to be doing, and try not to be self-conscious—forget yourself! Some nervousness is natural, especially the first time. Once you get into the experience, you'll probably drop all the stage fright in the spirit of worship. In other words, although the form is important if the worship service is truly to relate and communicate to people, once you've got a good idea what the form is, it should no longer hinder you. Remember, what is required of those who put the service together is a lot of expectation that something real is going to happen plus a commitment to it as worship.

This chapter has pointed out some of the ways barriers to worship experiences can be removed. These hints go together with the opening two chapters of the book. Without an understanding of what is meaningful in worship, you can flounder a long time trying to pick and choose the right combination. Similarly, if you don't put the service together in a way that will make it easy for the congregation, you can get in the way of a good experience.

In the two "additions" to the book that follow, you will find, first, examples of contemporary worship services that I wrote and that have proven meaningful; second, you will find a list of resources to get you farther down the road to writing your own worship service.

All that's left to be said at this point is . . .

Go in peace!

Create and celebrate!

4

First Addition:

Some of My Things

Following are some of one man's attempts to deal with the liturgy in terms meaningful for today. The things offered here are various. There are five different folk masses. You will see in them the bones of the liturgy outlined in chapter 2. There is one house-church eucharist, useful for small groups gathered in homes. One litany, used several times with teen-aged groups, seemed meaningful to them, so I have included it here. The two promised eucharistic prayers are here. I hope they praise the Lord! If these offerings nudge you to create your own services, they will have more than served their purpose.

A Folk Mass for Peace

Some Songs Maybe for Getting This Thing Started

"Blowin' in the Wind"

"Where Have All the Flowers Gone?"

We Prepare to Confront the Problem by Clearing the Boards with God

LEADER: In the Name of the Father and of the Son and of the Holy Ghost we begin our worship; in that Name we begin our lives; and in that Name we confront the need of the world for peace.

PEOPLE: Let our worship begin in his Name!

LEADER: Let us admit, brothers and sisters, that we have not come clean in this whole matter of being peacemakers. Let us admit there have been frequent times when we have been incapable of keeping or making peace with our brother on an individual, face-to-face, level. Let us admit that we have been so paralyzed by the sheer weight of the problems of the Middle East and of Vietnam that often we have shrugged them off, knowing not what to do, and eventually we have come to the point where we couldn't care less! Let us admit we have not done all we could, as individuals, and in our community of Christians, to realize peace and harmony among men. Let us take these problems to God.

PEOPLE: Father in heaven, whose will is for peace between individuals and among mankind's many nations, forgive us for hanging back when it comes to establishing your peace in our lives and in the world. Forgive us for believing we are too small to do any good; forgive us for believing that the problems will simply go away or eventually work themselves out without any help on our part; forgive us for not caring about the peace of God.

PASTOR: God hears your and my admissions. If you're ready to believe it, what he says in and through the cross and resurrection of Christ is for you! He says, forget the hang-ups of the past, turn over a new leaf, and begin again. That is the reason Christ lived, and that is the reason he died; to point us into a new life, and to give us the means to achieve it. The assurance of God's love and pardon is what the resurrection of Christ says to us. So I say to you that you *are* forgiven, and that you are now free to start again . . . free to start down the pathway to peace.

PEOPLE: Let it be so!

A HYMN OF ENTRANCE: "They'll Know We Are Christians"

We Enter the Presence of God to Hear the Word of Peace

ENTRANCE DECLARATION *(spoken by all):*
We're coming into your presence now, O Lord. We have made a clean sweep of the past, and we are now ready to leap into the future. But we need you and your word now, to give us the direction in which we must go. Come Lord Jesus, with your love and concern, and show us the love and concern we must have for the world. Show us your pathway of peace, O Christ, and help us to walk in it.

A HYMN OF GLORY: "Exaltation at the Coming of the Word"

THE WORD OF GOD FROM THE BIBLE: Isaiah 2:2–4; Matthew 5:38–48

THE WORD OF GOD REFLECTED IN TODAY'S WRITERS

THE RESPONSE IN CREED FORM: A sung version of the Apostles' Creed

LEADER: We have heard the word of God in old and new writings. We have given some response to this word through our confession of faith in the creed. We have still more to learn about peace from a contemporary word, but let us pause once more to sing praise to our Lord.

PEOPLE: We're beginning to get the message of peace. We hope this message will break through to us, and now we unite in song.

THE HYMN: "Lord of the Dance"

GOD'S WORD COMES THROUGH THE PREACHER: The sermon

We Respond to God's Word for Our Lives by Offering Ourselves to Him

(At this time, the offering is brought forward with the bread and the wine to show we are giving ourselves to God in the task of becoming peacemakers.)

THE OFFERING PRAYER *(spoken by all):*
Lord of the dance of life, Lord of all living things, whose will is for peace and not friction, who lived and died in order that we might have fullness of life, we offer ourselves to you as much as we can at the moment. We admit to a hanging mass of confusion in our lives; we admit we cannot often hear you speaking; but we have learned that your will is for peace,

and we offer ourselves humbly in the pursuit of peace in the world and in our private lives. Take this hesitant offering and do great things with it, O Lord, as you alone can do; take our hearts and minds and turn us to the pathway of peace, each in our own way, that the world may become a better place in which to live and love and enjoy. And now we pause in silence, that each of us here may open himself to God and, if he is so moved, share his thoughts with God and the whole community of love.

(Following silent prayer and vocal petitions the leader will conclude:) Take our offerings of coin and bread and wine, our offerings of prayer, praise, and thanksgiving, take ourselves as we are, O Lord, and through us work mighty things in the name of Christ and for the sake of peace. Amen.

A HYMN BEFORE COMMUNION: "Sons of God"

Christ Breaks through in the Bread and Wine of Holy Communion

LEADER: The Lord be with you.
PEOPLE: And with you, too.
LEADER: Let your hearts be raised in joy.
PEOPLE: We lift up our hearts joyfully to God.
LEADER: Let us thank the Lord, our God.
PEOPLE: It seems quite right to give thanks.
LEADER: It is quite right to give thanks to you, O God, Holy Father, for you have shown us the pathway to peace in the life of Jesus Christ our Lord; therefore with all of heaven and earth we give thanks to you for revealing your will to us, your people.

THE EUCHARISTIC PRAYER *(spoken by the pastor)*

THE LORD'S PRAYER *(in sung version)*

THE SHARING OF THE PEACE

LEADER: In token of our love for one another, our joy in life, and our continuing desire to spread peace to all mankind, we pass the peace of God among those gathered here. We pass this peace in token of the peace toward which we strive in life, in love with God and our fellowman, and in hope for a future under God which knows peace in all nations.

(The peace is passed through the congregation by the pastor and the musicians with the words "The Peace of the Lord be with you," to which you respond "Amen." The peace is then passed around the tables with the same words.)

THE HYMN BEFORE DISTRIBUTION: "In This Sacred Mystery"

THE DISTRIBUTION (During the distribution, the congregation will file past the communion table in single file to receive the bread and wine, then return to their seats.)

We Are Sent Back to the World to Establish Peace

LEADER: Give thanks to the Lord because he is good.

PEOPLE: And his love will last forever.

LEADER: Lord, you have come to us in the sign of forgiveness, in word and in sacrament and in this community. Help us to live out the reality of your Presence in our lives. Help us to become the peacemakers Christ intended us to be. Send us forth into the world, knowing that without you we cannot make peace, but with you we are able. Send us forth into the world, willing to do what we can, hoping for a peaceful and good future under you, and living with peace in our hearts toward others.

PEOPLE: Send us out, God, into the world in order that we may bring peace to the face of mankind and into the hearts of all we touch in the name and for the sake of Christ.

LEADER: The Lord be with you.

PEOPLE: And with you, too!

LEADER: Shall we bless the Lord once more?

PEOPLE: Yes, we'll bless him once again.

PASTOR: May the Lord bless you in the search for peace;
may he fill you with love wherever you go in life.
As he sends you forth in peace
may you spread this peace to each of the men
he sets before your path in life.

SHORT PERIOD OF SILENT PRAYER FOR PEACE

LEADER: Go, the mass is over! Now the work begins!

A Folk Mass for Joy in Life

WE GATHER TO SING PRAISE, REJOICING: "They Cast
Their Nets in Galilee"

*We Prepare Our Lives for Joy in Community with
Others*

LEADER: In the Name of the Father and of the Son and
of the Holy Ghost.

PEOPLE: That is how we must begin.

LEADER: People of God! Sometimes we hide the joy of
our faith under a bundle of excuses. Often we fail to
get the word from the cross and resurrection of Christ
that life is beautiful and that we are given time in
order to celebrate the gift of life. More often than we
wish, the whole point of Christianity—that God loves
us with a love that can change our dreary day-to-day
living into a wonderful experience of joy and inner
peace and unity with others—is lost. We get so involved in the crude pettiness of life that the big picture
of God's being in control, working to make all things
come out good for those who love him, is over-
shadowed. Let us confess these shortcomings in ourselves and let him put us together in joy again.

PEOPLE: God, we open our hearts to you:
We confess that we're not always ready for you;
We confess that we're not always joyful in life because
we forget you're with us;
We confess we often fail to take you seriously;
We confess that the sunshine of the resurrection is
often turned to rain in our hearts by our misunder-
standing and smallness of faith.

We believe a little, Lord, because each man has some beliefs by which he lives, whether he acknowledges them or not.

Help us to straighten out our beliefs and line them up with the cross and empty tomb, because we can't do that by ourselves—and we need that kind of belief to find real joy.

PASTOR: Let me remind you that God is in our midst at all times—wherever two or three people connect with each other in love and understanding. This is a clue from our side that joy and unity can be ours in life. But joy and unity are also things given in the cross and resurrection of Christ, and celebrated again and again in Holy Communion. God gives us joy in this life, and we must continually be aware of his unifying presence. If you can only accept this, we are ready to begin.

PEOPLE: So be it!

We Gather Joyfully as One in Christ

CHOIR SELECTION AS A DECLARATION OF ENTRANCE

THE GLORIA IN EXCELSIS IN FOLK SONG FORM

CHRIST COMES TO US IN THE WORD:
Some readings from the Bible on unity and joy
Some readings from today on joyful living

THE RESPONSE IN CREED: Sung version of the Apostles' Creed

THE HYMN: "When Jesus Came in Galilee"

CHRIST COMES TO US IN TODAY'S WORDS: The sermon

The Joyful Offering of Ourselves to God

AN OFFERING HYMN

THE OFFERTORY PRAYER *(spoken by all):*

We came here this evening, Lord, not at all sure what we would find. But we are learning through the story of your death and resurrection that we can be one with each other in the Spirit, and that we can rejoice in the midst of a world which is often not very joyful, because you are with us.

The only way we can show our thanks is by offering you a bit of ourselves, which we do at this time. Help us to offer more as we continue to grow in understanding; guide us forward into a committed, joyful, and fulfilling life. Take what we now offer, and change it from humility and commonness into uncommon greatness in your Supper. Amen.

THE SANCTUS IN FOLK SONG FORM

THE EUCHARISTIC PRAYER *(spoken by the pastor)*

THE TABLE GRACE OF THE CHURCH: A musical setting of the Lord's Prayer. (The Our Father is the "grace before meals" of the Christian church. It is a sign of solidarity in our approach to God.)

THE SHARING OF THE PEACE

LEADER: Our Lord says in Matthew's Gospel, "If you are offering your gift at the altar, and there remember that your brother has something against you, leave your gift there before the altar and go; first be reconciled with your brother, and then come and offer your gift." In token of our unity in Christ, our love for our brother, and as a sign of our fellowship, we shall pass the handshake through the congregation.

(The congregation will receive the handclasp at the end of each pew from the leaders with the words "The Peace of the Lord be with you," to which they should respond "Amen." Pass it in turn to your neighbor in the pew.)

THE COMMUNION HYMN: "Let Us Break Bread Together"

THE INVITATION TO JOIN CHRIST AT HIS TABLE

LEADER: Come to this table in peace and joy.
Come, not because you are strong but because you are weak.
Come, because you want to draw close to your fellowman in love and communication;
Come, because Christ is ready to meet you at his table to bring you joy and peace in this life and in the life to come.

THE DISTRIBUTION (During the distribution, the choir will sing softly several selections. Come to the altar rail, receive the loaf broken for you with the words "The Body of Christ, broken for you" and pass it to your neighbor on the left with the same words. The cup will be distributed by the pastor.)

We are Sent Back to the World in Joy

LEADER: We await, O Lord, your challenge to us to go back to the world as your servants.
PEOPLE: O God our Father, send us forth now,
sure of forgiveness for our sins;
sure of the freedom to be ourselves;
sure of joy and peace through life in Christ.

Send us out of this place—
> united one to another in faith;
> united one to another in hope;
> united one to another in love;
> united one to another in service to man;
> united one to another in and through your Son,
> Jesus Christ our Lord.

A FINAL HYMN OF JOY: "Allelu"

THE FINAL BLESSING:

LEADER: May the Lord break through to you.
PEOPLE: May he break through to you, too.
LEADER: Let's give thanks to God again.
PEOPLE: We certainly do thank him again.
LEADER: The Lord will bless you all;
> he can bring us all together
> as we learn he is our father.
> He can send us forth in joy,
> break the fears that us annoy.
> He assures us of his Presence
> as into life he sends us.
PEOPLE: And we end believing that he's with us all;
> for his joy and peace have come unto us all.

A Folk Mass for Freedom to Serve Others

AN OPENING SONG (selected for its relevance to the problem of freedom in today's world)

We Come before Our Heavenly Father, Seeking His Love for Our Lives

LEADER: We gather again in the Name and under the power and love of our God. He has created us in his image so that we may rise to the height of our power. Yet there are times when we fall under the burdens of life; there are times when we doubt the goodness and love of the God who made us and who gave us new life in Christ. Before we begin, then, let us come before God, asking that he will turn us on to life and to our responsibilities and possibilities as human beings, serving the world as his people.

PEOPLE: O Father, give us the mind of Christ that we may love, and the eyes of Christ that we may serve the world's need.

LEADER: Let us seek out God's will in order to do our ministry:

PEOPLE: God, we often fail to see the directions our lives should take. We fail for various reasons, not the least of which are fear and prejudice. Help us to follow Christ's guidance in the search for meaning in our lives and for the mission of the church.

LEADER: Let us seek to give ourselves to the world as servants and not as masters:

PEOPLE: God, you have given us the shape and style of your will in Jesus of Nazareth, who showed himself Lord in servanthood, and who received his authority by not being authoritarian. Help us all to see that the shape of his life must truly be the shape of our own, if the church is to survive and fulfill its mission through us now.

LEADER: Let us pray for sensitivity to the needs of the world:

PEOPLE: Sharpen our hearts, O God, to cut into the needs of our time;

Sharpen our ears, O Lord, to hear the cries of those who need your love and look for it to come through us;

Sharpen our minds, O Christ, that we may discover the mission of the church in respect to problems of race, war, poverty, hunger, and injustice;

Sharpen our faith, O Lord, that we may leave fear and cares behind and live on the edge of the world in the spirit of Christ and by the power of the Spirit.

LEADER: Let us seek the strength which God alone can give us in our need:

PEOPLE: Give us strength, God, as you break through to us anew in the words of Scripture, the book which creates and directs life;

Give us strength, God, as we remember our baptism as the means by which we were chosen to be your servants in the world and by which you first came to us as our loving Father;

Give us strength, God, through the proclamation of your love and acceptance of us in the absolution which frees us for life;

Give us strength, God, as Christ breaks through to us in his Supper and comes to gather us together

as one in him and one with each other, giving us
our daily bread that we may live his will;
Give us strength, God, through the love which our
Christian brothers bring us when we are beaten
and battered by our search to live for you in the
world you have given us.

PASTOR: In our seeking, we have realized how we fall
short of our Father's will, perhaps not intentionally,
but almost by accident. This falling short is part of
our shape as human beings, capable of things both
human and divine, both sinful and sinless. God has
given us the word that he will not hold our failures up
to our eyes, but will forgive and forget them in order
that we may be continually renewed and reopened
to the possibilities of life.

As a minister of the church of Christ, and by his
authority alone, I declare to you who have recognized
your failures the forgiveness of these failures in the
cross and resurrection of Jesus the Christ. Go forth
now, renewed, restored, and forgiven, that you may
once again serve God and man in free and loving
service.

PEOPLE: So be it!

*The Entrance of God's People into the Arena of
Freedom*

AN ENTRANCE HYMN *(sung by congregation and choir)*

THE SCRIPTURE READINGS:

LEADER: The first reading for this evening is a contemporary word in the form of a chancel drama. Here
God would speak to us in the concerns of the poet.

LEADER: The second readings for this evening come from God's word in the Scriptures. . . . Here end the readings.

PEOPLE: We give you thanks, O Lord.

THE CREEDAL RESPONSE: A sung version of the Nicene Creed

THE HYMN: "When Jesus Came in Galilee"

GOD COMES TO US IN THE WORDS OF TODAY: The sermon

We Present Our Lives to God That He May Work Through Us

(During the offering, the choir will sing a song that, it is hoped, will cause the congregation to reflect on its need to be committed to service in the world: "What Will I Do?"—a presentation of God's claim on our lives in blues form.)

THE PRAYER:

LEADER: Let us pray for everyone who is here:

PEOPLE: Listen to us, Lord!

LEADER: Let us pray for everyone who is not here:

PEOPLE: Listen to us, Lord!

LEADER: Let us pray for all men everywhere who are doing God's work:

PEOPLE: Listen to us, Lord!

LEADER: For everyone who is in bondage to wealth or to poverty:

PEOPLE: Listen to us, Lord!

LEADER: For everyone crushed because of race or ideology:

PEOPLE: Listen to us, Lord!

LEADER: For Christ's presence in everything we do:
PEOPLE: Listen to us, Lord!
LEADER: For all the many situations of life:
PEOPLE: Listen to us, Lord!
LEADER: For the freedom to do the will of God and make it truly our thing:
PEOPLE: Listen to us, Lord!

(Here the members of the congregation are asked to speak their individual petitions, cares, and intercessions, into the midst of the community; after a while, the leader will conclude:)

LEADER: Everything that we have said here, Father, in the community of love and trust, we offer to you: our hopes for the world, for the church, and for our individual lives we set before you; through Jesus Christ our Lord, who lives and rules with you, one God through all the ages.
PEOPLE: So be it!

THE OFFERTORY PRAYER *(spoken by all):*

Our heavenly Father, we are grateful that you have given us our daily bread in so many ways and by the hands of so many different people. We give back to you now a portion of this, that we may continually remind ourselves of our dependence on your loving care for all the good things of life. Let this portion be to us a sign of complete dedication to you; and remind us through the same that we are to turn outward to others in service under the freedom which is ours in Christ. Help us to remember, as we approach your table, that all things common are made holy when they are offered to you: our bread, our wine, our money, and especially our lives, in order that we may live freely toward others in love and service. This is clearly true!

Christ Comes to His Table to Bring Us Freedom to Serve Others

THE COMMUNION HYMN

THE EUCHARISTIC PRAYER *(by the pastor)*

THE LORD'S PRAYER: A sung version of the table grace of the people of God.

THE GIVING OF THE PEACE

LEADER: As a sign that nothing separates us from each other now that God has come with his love and forgiveness, and as a token of the embracing unity of all men in Christ, we now share the peace of God. We remember the words of John at this point, that no man can say "I love God" while at the same time hating his brother, and we rejoice that God has torn down the walls that separate us one from the other; in such a way is he freeing us to love the world with all its problems, wants, and needs.

(The peace is passed through the congregation with the words "The Peace of the Lord be with you," to which you should respond "Amen." Pass the peace with these words to the person nearest you.)

THE DISTRIBUTION

A POST-COMMUNION HYMN: "Lord of the Dance"

The Send-Off into Service to the World

LEADER: Lord, you have come to us again in the sign of forgiveness, in your word and in the sacrament. Help us to grab hold of these realities and to live out their meaning for our lives. Help us to become involved in the needs of this world, remembering that you got involved when you came among men in the form of a man, Jesus Christ our Lord. Thank you, Father, for the freeing, forgiving word both spoken and visible; send us forth now, refreshed and renewed, freed in Christ to serve.

PEOPLE: Send us forth, O Lord, to be your servants in the world, binding up the brokenhearted, caring for the sick of mind and body, challenging the evil of the world, and celebrating your forgiving presence in the nooks and crannies of everyday living.

LEADER: Let us thank the Lord once more.

PEOPLE: We will thank him once again.

PASTOR: May the grace of our Lord Jesus Christ free you for service; may the love of God cast out fear and give power to your lives; and may the fellowship of the Holy Spirit enable you to live on the raw edges of life, doing God's will.

PEOPLE: So be it!

A Christmas Folk Mass

ENTRANCE HYMN: "See the Baby Jesus" *(see page 82 for words and music)*

We Come before God to Lay Our Christmas Hang-Ups at the Door of His Heart

V. In the Name of the Father who began and continues the universe and who broke into our world in the Son who gives life and love, and in the Name of the Spirit who makes our community different from other groups, let us begin.

R. So be it!

V. Let us admit we have not approached this whole Christmas thing unspoiled by the commercialism and misguided nonsense that pretends to be the Christmas spirit.

R. Lord, we are sorry about the mess into which you've been put. Perhaps we should free you from the Christmas rush, but then we remember that you belong at the marketplaces of life, so perhaps it is not so bad after all, and you are surely free to be there, anyway. Only help us not to be smothered by the rush so that we no longer see you there.

V. But there is more. Each of us, when he is honest, will admit that he has already smothered Christ in the nostalgia and sentimentality of Christmases past and, worse, in his mind has locked him into the cradle at Bethlehem where, as a harmless baby, he cannot put many claims on us.

R. We admit we tend to see Christmas as a thing of the past and rarely get Christ out of the cradle to celebrate him as our Present and Coming Lord. We don't really mean to do this, but the way in which Christmas has been celebrated—the sentimental over-

SEE THE BABY JESUS

Moderately fast   Jay C. Rochelle

1. See   the ba - by   Je - sus, born in Beth - le - hem,
2. See   the child   Je - sus, in - side the tem-ple walls,
3. See   the grown man Je - sus, walk through Gal-i - lee;
4. See   the young man Je - sus hung at   Cal - va - ry;
5. See   the ris - en Je - sus break out from the grave;
6. Now   we no more see   him, yet he   is   a - round;

Born in or - der that all man-kind might be men a - gain,
talk with the es - tab - lish-ment deep with-in those halls,
feel his touch and hear his voice,and watch him set men   free.
feel the love that comes to men from him up - on the   tree;
he who died to free all men, him-self he would not save,
he is in the face of all the broth-ers we sur - round;

Scorned and walked by through his years, nev - er had man-y friends.
tell - ing them that God   is free, near to one and   all.
Watch his foot-steps, how   he walks straight to Cal-va - ry.
won - der why the world re - ject - ed him at thir-ty three.
so   that God the Fa - ther would be known by free and slave.
he   is   in   the love we feel wher-ev - er we are bound.

See the ba - by Je - sus, come to you a - gain.
See the child   Je - sus — can't you hear him call?
See the grown man Je - sus, free - ing you and me!
See the young man Je - sus — hung for you and me!
See the ris - en Je - sus break out from his cave!
Feel the ris - en Je - sus — in com-mun-ity he's found.

tones, the manger mentality—has played havoc with the truth that Christ is really present with us and not locked into the past.

V. The root problem is surfacing now, and it is this: often Christmas has no practical relationship to our lives. We celebrate it, but in such a way that it is a ball of fluff or a puff of smoke; one minute it is here, the next minute it is gone. When it doesn't challenge us to think about the fantastic love of God for man, and in turn consider what our response to this love in the world ought to be, then we are missing the point. The real crux of the matter comes when we can see Mary somehow in the unwed mother; when we can see Mary and Joseph in the black or Puerto Rican couple turned away from the doors of the houses of our city; when we can see the baby Jesus in the American Indian or Vietnamese child born into a degrading and dehumanizing environment. When we have begun to see the relationship between Christmas and the needs of the world, then Christmas has meaning for our lives.

R. These are hard words. We tend to think that we celebrate Christmas well when we sing the old carols and go through the traditional festivities and services. We pledge we will at least think on these hard sayings, and seek out *God's* meaning for Christmas rather than our own.

V. This being the case, I remind you that God is ready to forgive when we admit our wrongs, that his love is constant toward us even when we cannot feel it, and that Christ can continue to transform your life into one of celebration and service. Consider yourselves as those, then, who have been newly born into the love of God, and work from there into the true meaning of Christmas.

We Enter God's Presence to Hear His Word to Us in This Season

SPOKEN IN UNISON: We come into the Presence of the Christ who comes into our presence again in this Advent season. We look back with a joyous memory to his coming in history at Bethlehem; we look forward to his full Presence in love and joy at the end of time; and especially do we look now at his coming in word and in sacrament, in the faces of those in need, and in the love of the community which is his. Come, Lord Jesus!

THE KYRIE *(see page 85 for words and music)*

THE PRAYER TO GATHER OUR THOUGHTS *(in unison):*

Gather us together, O Lord, into the body of Christ in this place as we await our coming Lord. Grant us the vision of Christ's Presence in all of our lives and the peace which this brings. Show us your Presence, O God, in the dark and the light corners of life and at its very center, filling all of life with meaning and pointing us toward the future with love and hope; through Jesus Christ, our Lord, who lives and rules with you and the Spirit, one God, world without end. Amen.

A WORD FROM GOD THROUGH HIS WRITERS OF OLD

V. People of God! Prepare your hearts now to let God enter in as he comes in the word of Scripture.

R. We open our hearts to receive him and our ears to hear him.

KYRIE ELEISON!

Lively, with spirit   Jay C. Rochelle

★ Use third ending upon third repeat of "Kyrie"

The Lessons: Deuteronomy 18:15–19
John 1:19–28

A Word from God in the Writings of Today's
Prophets

V. People of God! Prepare your hearts now to let God
speak to you through those who write of life and
love today.

R. We open our hearts to receive him and our ears to
hear him.

THE APOSTLES' CREED

Moderate but not too slow   Setting by Jay C. Rochelle

I believe in God the Father, Maker of heaven and earth In Jesus Christ his Son our Lord; Con-ceived by the Holy Ghost, Born of the Virgin Ma—ry, Suffered under Pontius Pi—late, Crucified, dead, and bur—ied He descended into Hell; The third day he rose again from the dead; He as-cended into heaven, Sits at the right hand of God the Father; From thence he comes to judge the quick and the dead. I believe in the ho-ly Ghost; the Holy Christian Church, the Com-munion of Saints; the for-giveness of sins; the resurrection of the body; and the life everlasting. A-men.

The Readings from Now

V. Having heard God speaking to us as individuals and as his people, let us make our response to him in the singing of the creed.

THE APOSTLES' CREED *(see page 86 for words and music)*

THE SERMON HYMN: "People of God, Raise your Voices and Sing" *(see page 88 for words and music)*

GOD COMES TO US IN A CONTEMPORARY WORD: The sermon

We Offer Ourselves to God to Work the Miracle of Christmas through Our Lives

THE OFFERING

THE OFFERING PRAYER *(spoken by all):*

Heavenly Father, as we await with eager hearts the coming of Christ into our lives anew, we reflect on the meaning of Christmas: that you came into the world as a true person; that you came to bring peace and love; and that you came so men might recognize you as a God at hand and not far off. Help us recall that each of us must offer himself, as best he can, in the struggle to personalize your presence in the world. Remind us that Christ comes to men today through his church and that this ultimately means he comes through us as the people of God. We commit ourselves to you through our offerings of praise and thanks, and we offer ourselves to establish your truth and love in the world. We seek to follow Christ in making your love personal to all men. Amen.

Christ Comes to Us to Fill Our Lives with Joy and Meaning in His Supper

PEOPLE OF GOD, RAISE YOUR
VOICES AND SING

Jay C. Rochelle

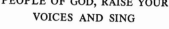

REFRAIN

Peo-ple of God, raise your voic-es and sing!

Shout, and let the whole cre - a-tion ring:

Na - ture and man - kind watch for their king.

Here we are, Lord, come!   Here we are, Lord, come!

1. We
2. We
3. We
4. You

seek you in the bus - y crowd - ed streets; we
see the world con-fused to the left and the right;
hear you in the word that comes from the cross;
live a - mong your peo - ple, your guid - ance you show;

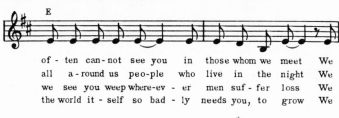

of - ten can - not see you   in   those whom we   meet   We
all   a - round us peo - ple   who   live in   the   night   We
we   see you weep wher-ev - er   men suf - fer   loss   We
the world it - self so bad - ly   needs you, to   grow   We

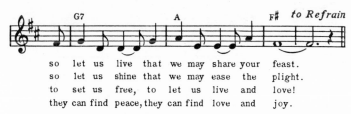

know that   you   are   com - ing   to   give   the   world   peace;
pray the world will   one   day   bask   in   your   light;
love you, Lord, be - cause you   paid   out   the   cost
are your peo - ple, and   we   must   let   all   men   know

so   let   us   live   that   we may   share your   feast.
so   let   us   shine   that   we may   ease   the   plight.
to   set   us   free,   to   let   us   live   and   love!
they can find   peace, they can find   love   and   joy.

THE COMMUNION HYMN: "Come, Lord Jesus" *(see page 90 for words and music)*

V. The Lord be with you.

R. And with you, too.

V. Let us lift up our hearts.

R. We lift them up in love for God.

V. Let us give thanks to God.

R. It is surely right to give him thanks.

V. It is surely right that we should everywhere and every time give thanks to God, the Holy Father, the all-powerful, eternal God, who has given his people strength through the promise of a Redeemer, through whom he will make all things new when he comes at the end of time, and through whom all things are now new for the people of God. So with angels, the

COME, LORD JESUS
(A Communion Hymn)

Lively with spirit (latin beat)   Jay C. Rochelle

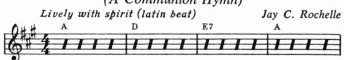

1. Come,— Lord Je - sus, and grace our ta-ble a - gain.
2. Come, ris - en Lord, —— and bring your pres-ence to - day.
3. Come, pres-ent Christ,— and us your word de - clare,

Stand-ing in your pres - ence, we're joined by fel - low men.
We who eat this bread and wine need a guide for the way.
spo - ken and in - vis - i - ble, let us one and all share

Shar - ing in your fes-tive meal, we re - new our hearts,
We who stand to - geth - er ask of you to give
in the com-mon fes - ti - val giv'n for us to eat,

we who come to - geth - er, — one from man - y parts
us your lov - ing pres - ence_ so that we may live.
that we see in neigh-bors the Christ we wish to meet.

Come,— Lord Je - sus, and grace our ta-ble a - gain.__
Come, ris-en Lord,— and bring your pres-ence to - day.__
Come,— O Christ, that in your love we share__

whole host of heaven and earth, we honor his name, giving praise to him and saying:

R. Holy, holy, holy, Lord God of hosts; Heaven and earth are full of your glory; Hosanna in the highest.

Blessed is he who comes in the Name of the Lord; Hosanna in the highest.

THE LORD'S PRAYER *(see page 92 for words and music)*

THE PRAYER OF THANKSGIVING

V. We'll learn, God:

R. We'll learn to live Christmas all year.

V. We'll learn to laugh and sing:

R. We'll learn to celebrate life.

V. We'll learn to hear you calling everywhere:

R. In the words of Scripture and of the poet;
   In the sacraments of the church;
   In the community of the people of God;
   In the needs of the world.

V. We'll learn to praise you everywhere:

R. In the mills of the city;
   In the midst of the farmlands;
   In the social gaiety and in the lonely quiet of life;
   In times of stillness and in times of noise.

V. But now let us pass into prayer, O Lord:

R. Let us bring you our tight-lipped words of despair;
   Let us tell you our songs of hope and joy;
   Let us bring you the puzzles and problems of our lives.
   Hear us, O Lord, as we speak hesitantly and haltingly,
   Bringing you the things we need to say, that you need to hear.

(Here a period of silence will be observed that individuals may speak their needs to God in the circle of love and concern.)

THE OUR FATHER

Jay C. Rochelle

thine is the king-dom, and the pow'r, and the glo - ry, for - ev - er.____ A - men. A - men. A - men.____

V. All these things we wrap up as our gift of love, faith, and thanks to you, O God. Accept them and us in our honesty.

THE EUCHARISTIC PRAYER *(by the pastor)*

THE GIVING OF THE PEACE

V. People of God, who await the coming Christ now and always, let us show the world the peace we have among ourselves. In token of our love for one another, our joyful expectation, and our desire to celebrate the reconciling Presence of Christ in all of life, we pass the peace of God to all gathered here. We pass this peace in love for God and for fellowmen, in hope for an open future under God, and as a sign of the Presence of our coming Lord.

(The peace will be passed throughout the congregation with the words "The Peace of the Lord be with you," to which you reply "And with you, too." Those on the ends of the pews receiving the peace will then turn to those next to them and pass it, and so on across the pews.)

THE AGNUS DEI *(see page 94 for words and music)*

THE DISTRIBUTION (Please wait for instructions.)

We Are Sent Back to the World in Love and Hope

AGNUS DEI

Moderate with feeling   Jay C. Rochelle

O Christ, thou Lamb of God, who takes a-way the sin of the world, have mer-cy. O Christ, thou Lamb of God, who takes a-way the sin of the world, have mer-cy ____ O Christ, thou Lamb of God, who takes a-way the sin of the world, grant us thy peace. ____ A - men. ____

V. Give thanks to our good God.

R. Because his love is constant.

POST-COMMUNION PRAYER *(said by all):*

We give you great thanks, O Lord, that you have given us the cup of joy and the bread of peace which refresh and restore us to new life. We ask you to strengthen us, through this gift, in faith toward you, in deep community love toward one another, in patience in the midst of the problems of life, and in the hope of life eternal; through Jesus Christ, your Son, our Lord, who lives and rules with you and the Holy Spirit, one God, world without end. Amen.

V. The Lord be with you.

R. And with you, too.

V. Let us bless the Lord again.

R. Yes, we'll bless him once more!

V. May the Lord who comes at Christmas in word and sacrament,

who comes in the world in the form of love and caring,

who comes at the end of time to gather all men to himself,

give you eve.y blessing and the mind to follow his will

as you go through life one of his people.

R. So be it!

V. Go! The Mass is over; let the service begin!

Folk Mass for the Care of the Earth

The following folk mass is a celebration of concern for the environmental problems of our nation, of our world, of our earth. It is an entirely new production, especially for use in connection with "Care of the Earth Day" of the Allentown Area Council of Churches. Many who will be in this celebration have been involved for months in the planning of "Care of the Earth Day." We give thanks for them individually and as a group. Many here tonight marched on the trash trek this afternoon to gain funds for the Lehigh River Restoration Association. All offerings in this evening's folk mass will go to the same organization. We give thanks for the marchers. Let's celebrate!

A SONG FOR BEGINNING: "Clap Your Hands"

LEADER: Let us begin, in the Name of the God who created the world and all who live in it, the God who sustains this creation and saves it from itself, and the God who infuses it with power and love.

PEOPLE: Let it be so!

LEADER: Here we are again, God, unsure of our position in your eyes, unsure of where we stand with each other, unsure of our relationship with your world. We come together simply because we care about the earth. It has given us life; we owe it something. We have become aware of its problems, the problems that we have laid upon it. We have met the enemy, and he is within us. We have heard the scream of the butterfly. And now we stand in your Presence, sorry that we have not acted before.

PEOPLE: We confess our sorrow to each other and to God for not having opened our eyes to the problems of the earth until this time, for not having spoken or acted on behalf of our mother earth, for not recognizing in the work of the unsung few a work of environmental control which should be our own. We acknowledge our awkwardness in not knowing exactly how to begin, where to go to help, how to sensitize others to the problems. But we pledge honesty and integrity in this cause, which we today make truly our own.

LEADER: The God who is not afraid to roll up his sleeves and become involved in dirt and grass, flowers and fields, fire and water, hears your confession. He invites you to forget your past errors of judgment, your past omissions of concern, and join with him in the protection and preservation of the earth. He invites you to rise up as trustees of the earth and not its masters, as users and not abusers of nature, as stewards of the mysteries of creation in field or test tube, stone or brook. He calls you back to sensitivity to the needs of creation, and he says to you today, "You are free to take charge, in responsibility, of the earth which I have given you to till and to love." Go with this assurance ringing in your ears; come together now to celebrate your concern!

PEOPLE: We hear this word for our lives, and we will come and go with it. We stand now, prepared to sing and dance and to come together in union with our brothers. We are free. We are in the liberated zone, the zone of love and concern, the zone where God is to be found!

AN ANTHEM TO BRING US TOGETHER IN CONCERN: "This Is My Father's World"

THE READINGS

LEADER: Listen, people, with open ears, to the words of old wise times speaking to us of God's world!

PEOPLE: Bring us the word!

(Leader reads the Bible lesson.)

LEADER: Listen, people, with open ears, to the words of young thoughtful men speaking to us of God's world!

PEOPLE: Bring us the word!

(Leader reads the lesson from contemporary literature.)

THE AFFIRMATION *(spoken by all in unison):*

This is God's earth.
We are stewards of that earth.
We know we have abused the earth.
We try to love the earth.
This is God's earth, and he loves it.
We are God's people, and he loves us.
We ask him to help us love the earth more.
We live in the asphalt world.
We find it hard to tune in to the earth.
We fail to see, sometimes, the need
to smell a spring flower,
or skip a stone over water,
or feel the mud between our toes on rainy days.
We are out of touch with the earth.
Help us, God, to be sensitive to the earth.
We are here because we want to be sensitive.
We have made the first step.
We have recognized the earth.
With you, O God, we walk the earth,
sensing its real needs,
sensing our need to be in tune with it.
We are potential caretakers
trying to be actual caretakers.
We feel your Presence with us, O Lord,
as we care for the earth.

HYMN: Psalm 98, to the tune of "Swing Low, Sweet Chariot"

MIXED MEDIA SERMON

1. Presentation of "Pollution in the Valley," by the Charles Snelling family—filmstrip and tape recording;

2. Discussion of filmstrip in pews. (When the film-strip is over, simply turn to your neighbor in the pew and discuss its meaning for you.)

THE LITANY FOR THE CARE OF THE EARTH *(congregation standing)*

LEADER: For all the gifts of rain and sun, for the pro-duce of the land, for seasonal foliage, and for the crops we harvest:
PEOPLE: Lord, we give you thanks.
LEADER: For all the many ways in which we have learned to use the raw materials of the earth and for the people who manufacture for us:
PEOPLE: Lord, we give you thanks.
LEADER: For the ability to come into contact with the earth, to smell its richness and feel its warmth and cold, to dance like Zorba, united with nature:
PEOPLE: Lord, we give you thanks.
LEADER: For the answers to the great problems of pol-lution and degradation of our water, land, and air:
PEOPLE: We seek the Spirit's help.
LEADER: For sensitivity to uncover the ways in which we might fight the special problems of our area in pollution and degradation:
PEOPLE: We seek the Spirit's help.

(Here the litany becomes "free form"; each individual is invited to speak loudly his own *special* concern in the presence of the total congregation. As individuals be-gin to speak, the congregation continues to respond, "We seek the Spirit's help." After a number of minutes have gone by and people have made known their needs, the leader will conclude:)

LEADER: These are our concerns, Lord. Help us to tune in to them in whatever way we can. Help us to combat those who would destroy and denude our earth. Bring us together in a body of concern, as we seek to care for the earth.

PEOPLE: Let it be so!

THE OFFERING: Bread and wine and money to celebrate our concern

OFFERING ANTHEM: "The Lord of My Life"

OFFERING PRAYER *(spoken by all):*

God of stone and flower, God of rain and sunshine, God of the butterfly and the bear, God of asphalt paving and mountain slope, we offer ourselves to you. Take us and these gifts of bread and wine and money and use them to the best of our ability and the fullness of your need. We pledge ourselves to partnership with you in the fight to care for the earth. Accept us as we are, knowing our weakness. Work through us to strengthen us in our concern, our words, and our action. Walk with us in the garden in the cool of the day, as you did with our first parents. Help us to guide the spaceship earth, our first and only home. Accept our offering in love as you accept us through love. Amen.

OFFERING HYMN: "What Have They Done to the Rain?"

THE FESTIVE MEAL OF GOD'S PEOPLE

LEADER: God be with you!
PEOPLE: And with you, too!
LEADER: Let your joy and festivity raise up!
PEOPLE: We raise it up to God!

LEADER: Let us give thanks to God.

PEOPLE: It is surely right to give thanks.

LEADER: It is surely right to give thanks anywhere, anytime, to God our Creator. In our moments of deep sensitivity, the doors of perception in our minds unlock and we realize ourselves to be part of a flow of energy and love which is not of our own making, but into whose stream we step.* We see our union with each other and with nature all in a bright flash, and we strive to realize that union at all times, knowing it is given by God. Therefore with all heaven and earth, with all powers seen and unseen, we render our praise and thanks by saying:

PEOPLE: Holy, holy, holy, Lord God of Hosts; Heaven and earth are full of your glory; Hosanna in the highest. Blessed is he who comes in the Name of the Lord; Hosanna in the highest.

A EUCHARISTIC PRAYER FOR THE CARE OF THE EARTH *(by the pastor)*

THE LORD'S PRAYER *(in unison)*

THE PEOPLE'S PEACE:

LEADER: As a sign that we are in tune with each other, that we sense our needs as individuals and as a people, that we are joined by our concern for the care of the earth, let us now pass the sign of peace among all our brothers and sisters gathered here.

(The peace will be passed from the celebrant to the ushers, who will in turn pass it to the end person in the pews with the words, "Peace be with you," to which you respond, "And with you, too." The end

* This thought reflects the Eucharistic Prayer of the Free Church of Berkeley, California.

person then passes the peace to the next person in the pew, and so on through the pew.)

THE EUCHARISTIC HYMN: "Here We Are"

DISTRIBUTION OF THE MEAL TO THE PEOPLE OF GOD

(Instructions for the distribution: Beginning with the first pew on the righthand side of the church—facing the altar—the people will simply file out and come up and around the freestanding altar and there receive the bread and wine of the Holy Meal. Continuing around the table, return to your seats by the side aisle.)

THE BLAST-OFF INTO THE WORLD

LEADER: Give thanks to the Lord, for he is good.

PEOPLE: And his goodness will last forever.

LEADER: We give thanks to you, O God, that you have refreshed us through this sacred meal, and we ask you to bless us as individuals and as a group, both now and in the future, through the meal we have just received. Bind us together in concern; lift our hearts above the commonplace; and set our minds on the pattern of Christ the Liberator.

PEOPLE: Let it be so!

LEADER: The Lord be with you.

PEOPLE: And with you, too.

LEADER: Shall we bless the Lord once more?

PEOPLE: Yes, we bless him one last time.

LEADER: Go in power and peace.

Go, strengthened to confront the problem.

Go to serve the Lord in all things.

Remember your freedom!

RECESSIONAL HYMN: "Wonder-full World" (*As you leave the pews, go singing and moving to the hymn.*)

A House-Church Eucharist:
The Work and Words of Worship

We Prepare Our Lives for Worship

PASTOR: In the Name of the Father who loves us, the Son who has freed us, and the Holy Spirit who gathers us together.

PEOPLE: Amen.

PASTOR: I confess to Almighty God and to you, my brothers, that I have sinned in thought, word, and deed. I have turned aside from God at many points in my life. Therefore I ask you as fellow Christians to ask God for my forgiveness through Jesus Christ, our Lord.

PEOPLE: May Almighty God keep on loving you, forgive you your sin, turn you back to him, and lead you to a fulfilled and whole life.

PASTOR: Amen.

PEOPLE: I confess to Almighty God and to you, brother, that I have sinned in thought, word, and deed. I have turned aside from God at many points in my life. Therefore I ask you as a brother in Christ to ask God for my forgiveness through Jesus Christ, my Lord.

PASTOR: May Almighty God keep on loving you, forgive you your sin, turn you back to him, and lead you to a fulfilled and whole life.

PEOPLE: Amen.

We Gather as One in Christ

AN ENTRANCE DECLARATION *(spoken by all):*

As the broken bread was scattered over the mountains and was gathered together and became one, so let your church be gathered together from the ends of the earth into your kingdom. As we gather for our worship, Lord, let us become one with you and with one another, because you have made us one through the cross and the resurrection. Glory be to the Father, and to the Son, and to the Holy Ghost: as it was in the beginning, is now and ever shall be, world without end. Amen.

PASTOR: The Lord be with you!

PEOPLE: And with you, too!

THE SCRIPTURE READINGS

THE CREEDAL RESPONSE

THE MEDITATION

We Offer Ourselves to God

OFFERING OF THE ELEMENTS FOR HOLY COMMUNION BY HEAD OF HOUSE

OFFERING PRAYER *(spoken by all):*

Take this bread and this wine, Lord, as symbols of all that we are and have and all that we hope to be. Remind us through them that we are offering ourselves—our homes, our jobs, our studies, our play— to you that, through the cross and resurrection and in Holy Communion, they may be given back to us set apart and useful for your purposes in this world and the next.

OFFERING HYMN

God-in-Christ Comes to Us in Holy Communion

THE EUCHARISTIC PRAYER

THE LORD'S PRAYER

THE SHARING OF THE PEACE

PASTOR: Our Lord Jesus Christ says in Matthew, "If you are offering your gift at the altar, and there remember that your brother has something against you, leave your gift there before the altar and go: first be reconciled with your brother, and then come and offer your gift." In token of our unity in Christ and of our love for our brother, and as a sign that there is no ill will between us, let us now shake hands with those to the right and the left of us.

(People will respond with the handclasp.)

A COMMUNION HYMN

THE DISTRIBUTION (When passing the bread, say, "N., the Body of Christ, broken for you"; when passing the cup, say, "N., the blood of Christ, shed for you." Those receiving please respond, "Amen.")

We Go into the World Strengthened by Christ

THE SEND-OFF *(said by all):*

Lord, make us go into your world accompanied by your peace to live according to your word; for you have opened our eyes to the joy of being one in Christ and one with each other, the joy that you planned for all men to have. Lead us forth now, refreshed and strengthened, to bring that joy to all men.

PASTOR: The Lord be with you.

PEOPLE: And with you, too!

THE BENEDICTION

A Litany on the Creed for Teens

This litany can be done by one person with congregational response, but it is better to use two or three readers. This is marked in the text: *1, 2,* and *3* are readers, *R* is congregation.

1: Lord, I want to be dead to the need to help you provide for, preserve, and protect your world.

R: I believe in God the Father Almighty, Maker of heaven and earth.

2: But I don't care about that! Let me stay in a corner by myself. I don't want to be involved in this world, God, because it costs too much. I might actually have to do something. I might even have to speak about you . . . even in school!

R: I believe that God has created me and all that exists. He has given me and still provides me with food and clothing, home and family, daily work, and all I need from day to day. God also protects me in time of danger and guards me from every evil.

3: But, God, I can't buy that. I brush my teeth, I bathe myself, I play it cool with my health. You don't have anything to do with that. I go out and buy what I need when I need it. I don't need you for *that,* God!

R: All this he does out of fatherly and divine goodness and mercy, though I do not deserve it. Therefore I ought surely to thank and praise, serve and obey him. This is most certainly true.

2: Let me alone, God. Let me keep thinking I run my life. Don't make life any harder for me than it is. Don't ask me to take responsibility in a world other people have loused up. Let me stay dead, Lord. I don't want to serve and obey you!

R: I believe in Jesus Christ his only Son our Lord, Who was conceived by the Holy Ghost, Born of the Virgin Mary, Suffered under Pontius Pilate, Was crucified, dead, and buried: He descended into hell; The third day he rose again from the dead; He ascended into heaven, And sitteth on the right hand of God the Father Almighty; From thence he shall come to judge the quick and the dead.

1: There you go again, God. You're asking me to believe all that *extra* stuff. Sure, I believe in you, God. Doesn't everybody? Why, I can find you in nature. I know you forgive me, God. That's your job, isn't it? So don't ask me to buy all that stuff about Jesus, too!

R: I believe that Jesus Christ—true God, son of the Father from eternity, and true man, born of the Virgin Mary—is my Lord. He has redeemed me, a lost and condemned creature, saved me at great cost from sin, death, and the power of the devil—not with silver and gold, but with his holy and precious blood and his innocent suffering and death.

3: Why would anybody want to die for another person, God? Sounds ridiculous. Then you're trying to tell us that this Jesus is the one who gives *us* new life. No thanks, God! I'd rather be dead the way I am, and hang on to my cool, and not have to put my trust in something like that. No thanks, God. I'd rather be dead.

R: All this he has done that I may be his own, live under him in his kingdom, and serve him in everlasting righteousness, innocence, and blessedness, just as he is risen from the dead and lives and rules eternally. This is most certainly true.

3: Wait a minute, God. You're not serious about me
serving him and living under him? That's asking too
much, God! Why can't you just hang off the edge of
the world and leave *my* world alone? Why do you
have to come tampering around, trying to change
people? People like me, Lord—well, we just want to
stay dead—if being alive in a real way means to serve
Jesus.

R: I believe in the Holy Ghost; the holy Christian
Church, the Communion of Saints; The Forgiveness
of sins; The Resurrection of the body, And the Life
everlasting. Amen.

2: Some of that sounds okay, God! But you had to go
and throw in those corny things again, like the "holy
Christian Church." Man, I've been to church! Who
are you trying to put on? Those people there in
church are out of it. They are putting you on sometimes, God. They're a bunch of hypocrites who put
on a mask of piety for a few hours on Sunday. They're
dead most of the time. At least, they're dead according to what you're trying to tell me.

R: I believe that I cannot by my own understanding
or effort believe in Jesus Christ, my Lord, or come to
him. But the Holy Spirit has called me through the
gospel, enlightened me with his gifts, and sanctified
and kept me in the true faith. In the same way he
calls, gathers, enlightens, and sanctifies the whole
Christian church on earth, and keeps it united with
Jesus Christ in the one true faith.

3: Yeah, now you're making sense, God. I believe that
I cannot by my own understanding believe, either.
So that's not bad. But then how *can* I believe, God,
the way you've been talking to me? Through the

Holy Spirit, you say? But where can I find the Holy Spirit?

R: In this Christian church day after day he fully forgives my sins and the sins of all believers. On the last day he will raise me and all the dead and give me and all believers in Christ eternal life. This is most certainly true.

1: Hey, maybe that's really it. "In this Christian church . . ." Maybe I've been so busy looking at the hypocrites that I couldn't find the *real* people. And that's what it's all about, isn't it, Lord? I mean, when two people really get together, you're there with that forgiveness you're talking about, right? Hey, maybe there *is* something going on here. Make me come alive, God. I've been dead!

R: Just as he is risen from the dead and lives and rules eternally.

1: Death or life! Which one do I really want more? Life costs more!

R: Behold, I set before you this day death or life. Therefore choose life . . . freedom . . . forgiveness . . . and a new purpose in life, to live for Christ in God's world as yourself.

2: That's it! Life is mine to grab hold of and run with. God buys me as I am. I'm free. I'm free to live with and for others!

All: Help us, O God, not to believe only but to *do* your word. Help us to love and care and help in your world, because your Son died our death in order that we might live his life. Help us to come alive to each other and to the world. Amen.

A Eucharistic Prayer for Peace

God of all people and all places, God of love and hope, God who loves and cares for *us,* we pause simply to give you thanks. Most of the time we are in the world, getting crushed often, occasionally hitting a few high peaks, just living along as best we can. But we want to pause now especially to thank you. We thank you first of all for the world; we really love it, with all its problems. We get much from it, and we should return much to it. Thank you for the friends we have who love us as we are, particularly those within the community of the church. We give you thanks, too, for the peacemakers who have shown the way: for gentle Saint Francis of Assisi; for good Pope John; for John and Robert Kennedy; for Mahatma Gandhi and for Martin Luther King, Jr.; for all who have tried to show the pathway to peace and unity among men, we give you thanks, O God.

Most of all, we give you thanks for Jesus Christ, our brother and savior. When we stop for a moment, we recognize how, through Christ, you love and trust us, despite our failures which pinch and hurt us because they must pinch and hurt you, too. We do give you thanks for your powerful love and your close communion with us.

Especially do we now recall the life, death, and resurrection of Christ our Lord; we remember how much he loved all men and how he destroyed evil by his intensively good and loving nature. We remember that he conquered death as a sign to us that we too may conquer it, and as a display of the will and the peace of

God to the world. We remember the night before he died, when he gathered his small band together and, out of love for them and for a hostile world roundabout him, took bread, and when he had given thanks, broke it and gave it to them, saying, "Take, eat; this is my Body." Likewise he took the cup and, when he had drunk from it, gave it to them, saying, "All of you drink this. It is the blood of the new covenant, shed for you for the forgiveness of sins." In such a way he comes to us today with the message of peace and brotherhood, able to work this miracle through us.

And so we call for the Spirit of God, who leads men into all the truth and into the community of love and trust we call the church, to be with us today. Take these offerings, this bread and this wine, take our selves and use them as tools for the performance of your will in the world. We recognize our limitations too well; work through our strengths, and through our weaknesses, too. Draw us together in love; give us the means to make peace in this Holy Meal, and send us forth set apart for God's purposes in the world. Now may all glory and honor, praise and thanksgiving, love and power, be to God the Father, Son, and Holy Ghost forever and ever. Amen.

A Eucharistic Prayer for the Care of the Earth

We give thanks to you, O God, for all the many gifts you have given us. But we stand ashamed before you for the many ways we have bent nature out of sorts and destroyed its beauty and health-giving properties. We are sick when we see the smog that destroys your air; we are sick when we see the destruction of natural wonders in the name of progress. We confess our sorrow over that. We give thanks for your creation, but we also give pause to consider how badly it has been treated, and to assume our responsibility for this destruction, either by being directly involved or by our quiet assent to its occurrence. We offer to you not these cursed actions of man, but the achievements we have made within the framework of our harmony with nature. We offer our conquering of disease, our reaching to the depths of the sea and the vast heights of space. Take these as part of man's thanksgiving for the creation, and make us ever keener to the destructive forces we must now control to tend your creation as you want it tended.

We give thanks now for that great caretaker of man and nature, Jesus Christ the Second Adam. We see in him the answer to the puzzle of man's relationship to nature, the answer to God's use of manufactured products for his will, and the answer to man's harmony with his fellowman. On the night when he was betrayed, he took bread and gave thanks. Then he broke it and gave it to his disciples, saying, "Take and eat; this is my Body." In the same fashion he took the cup, drank from it, and gave it to them, saying, "Drink from it, all of you; for this cup is the new testament in my blood, shed for you for the forgiveness of sins." By so doing, besides reestablishing man's broken fellowship with God, he also reestablished man's proper care of the earth in stewardship under God; he showed that man is the trustee, not the master, of creation. He showed that the creation turns against man when it is abused, and he showed us the desire of God which enables us to use the creation rightly for our purposes and his. As we partake of this meal, O God, remind us of our proper relationship with nature, shown us in the figure of Jesus Christ our Lord.

Send your Spirit into our midst that we may become one in Christ and with each other. Take this bread and wine and use them for your purposes in the world; take us and use us as stewards of the creation, in order that in all things the whole world may sing praise to you. And now to God the Father, Son, and Holy Spirit be all glory and honor, world without end. Amen.

5

Second Addition:

Lots of Resources

BACKGROUND MATERIAL ON THE CHURCH
IN THE TWENTIETH CENTURY

(The following books can be read to get some idea of the concept of the church, its mission, and the place of the laity today.)

Berton, Pierre. *The Comfortable Pew*. Philadelphia: Lippincott, 1965. ($3.50; paperback, $1.95.)

By a lapsed Canadian Anglican. Critical of the church. Very good, but fails to consider much movement toward reform in the church already in existence.

Bliss, Kathleen. *We the People: A Book about Laity*. Philadelphia: Fortress, 1964. (Paperback, $1.75.)

Good study of the ecumenical movement and its relation to the laity as the whole "people of God."

Bonhoeffer, Dietrich. *Life Together*. New York: Harper & Row, 1954. ($2.50.)

A beautiful study of the meaning of the church as community.

Boyd, Malcolm, ed. *The Underground Church*. Baltimore: Penguin, 1969. (Paperback, 95¢.)

Essays from the underground.

De Dietrich, Suzanne. *The Witnessing Community: The Biblical Record of God's Purpose.* Philadelphia: Westminster, 1958. ($3.75.)

A magnificent study of the biblical record of God's purpose in history and specifically within the church.

Furlong, Monica. *With Love to the Church.* Forward Movement Miniature Books.

A loving but critical look at the frustrations one British laywoman faced finding acceptance of herself in a dogmatic church.

Gibbs, Mark, and Morton, T. Ralph. *God's Frozen People: A Book for and about Christian Laymen.* Philadelphia: Westminster, 1965. (Paperback, $1.65.)

A classic study on the laity and its disenfranchisement in the church.

Kraemer, Hendrik. *A Theology of the Laity.* Philadelphia: Westminster, 1959. ($3.00.)

The "original" in a long series of books dedicated to recapturing the biblical notion of the *Laos* ("people") as the total body of those who minister.

Raines, Robert A. *New Life in the Church.* New York: Harper & Row, 1961. ($3.95.)

A Methodist clergyman tells of revitalization of his church.

Robinson, John A. T. *Honest to God.* Philadelphia: Westminster, 1963. (Paperback, $1.65.)

The classic work in an era of breakthroughs in contemporary theology. Uneven, but still good for thought-provoking discussion.

——. *On Being the Church in the World.* Philadelphia: Westminster, 1962. ($3.50.)

Thirteen essays, the best of which speak of the relevance of the gospel to politics, race, and health.

——. *The New Reformation.* Philadelphia: Westminster, 1965. (Paperback, $1.65.)

Contains a good section on developing a genuine lay theology, which obliterates the "clergy-lay" distinctions.

Rose, Stephen C., ed. *Who's Killing the Church?* New York: Association, 1966. (Paperback, $1.50.)

A clot of essays dedicated to the proposition that most of the organizations and structures of the contemporary church, far from enabling it to minister to the world, *thwart* such ministry.

Spike, Robert Warren. *In but Not of the World: A Notebook of Theology and Practice in the Local Church.* New York: Association, 1957. (Out of print; check your library.)

Through a series of vignettes, the author helps laymen understand their place as ministers and "priests," the concept of the body of Christ, and the authority of the word for the church. Published for the Interseminary Commission of the National Council of Churches.

Webber, George W. *God's Colony in Man's World.* Nashville: Abingdon, 1960. ($2.75; paperback, $1.25.)

A theological study of the East Harlem Protestant Parish. Good for all churches grappling with their relevance.

Williams, Colin A. *Where in the World?* and *What in the World?* New York, National Council of Churches. (Out of print; check your library.)

Companion volumes which were blockbusters of Christian radical thinking when first issued.

HEAVY BACKGROUND ON THE LITURGY AND LITURGICAL RENEWAL

(The following books give a good background in understanding the liturgy. Unfortunately, most of them are technical, and uninteresting for those not tuned in.)

Aulén, Gustaf. *Eucharist and Sacrifice*. Philadelphia: Muhlenberg, 1958. (Out of print; check your library.)

A classic work on the connection between Holy Communion and the one work of Christ on the cross.

Brilioth, Yngve. *Eucharistic Faith and Practice, Evangelical and Catholic*. Naperville, Ill.: Allenson, 1930. ($6.00.)

Another classic work.

Brown, Edgar S., Jr. *Living the Liturgy*. Philadelphia: Fortress, 1961. (Paperback, $1.75.)

A lively little book written to help people understand the meaning of the Lutheran Sunday Communion service.

Davis, Charles. *Liturgy and Doctrine*. New York: Sheed & Ward, 1961. ($2.50.)

Roman Catholic study of the connection between the Mass and Catholic doctrine.

Dix, Gregory. *The Shape of the Liturgy.* 2nd ed. Naperville, Ill.: Allenson, 1945. ($10.00.)

A classic work that is a standard in the field of liturgical knowledge.

Herrlin, Olof. *Divine Service: Liturgy in Perspective.* Philadelphia: Fortress, 1966. ($3.75.)

A very deep, rich, and rewarding study of the theological meaning of worship in the Lutheran tradition.

Koenker, Ernest B. *Worship in Word and Sacrament.* St. Louis: Concordia, 1959. (Paperback, $1.50.)

An early work in Lutheran liturgical renewal; still quite good.

Maxwell, William D. *An Outline of Christian Worship: Its Development and Forms.* New York: Oxford University Press, 1939. ($4.25.)

A good study of worship patterns from a Presbyterian viewpoint.

Reed, Luther D. *Worship: A Study of Corporate Devotion.* Philadelphia: Fortress, 1959. ($5.95.)

A monumental work in the field.

———. *The Lutheran Liturgy.* Rev. ed. Philadelphia: Fortress, 1960. ($11.00.)

Another monumental work, in the limited field of Lutheran worship.

Robinson, John A. T. *Liturgy Coming to Life.* Philadelphia: Westminster, 1964. (Paperback, $1.45.)

A study of the renewal of worship at Clare College, where the bishop was once in residence.

Shepherd, Massey H., Jr., ed. *The Eucharist and Liturgical Renewal.* New York: Oxford University Press, 1960. ($3.00.)

A report of proceedings at the Liturgical Conference held at San Antonio in 1959.

———. *The Liturgical Renewal of the Church.* New York: Oxford University Press, 1960. (Out of print; check your library.)

This and the preceding volume offer a lot to even the occasional reader.

Thurian, Max. *The Eucharistic Memorial.* Part 1: *The Old Testament;* and Part 2: *The New Testament.* Richmond: John Knox, 1961. (Paperback, $2.25 each.)

Good biblical study.

Vajta, Vilmos. *Luther on Worship.* Philadelphia: Fortress, 1958. ($4.50.)

Precisely what the title suggests. Lots of meat here to chew on.

BOOKS USEFUL FOR CONTEMPORARY WORSHIP

Boyd, Malcolm. *Are You Running with Me, Jesus?* New York: Holt, Rinehart & Winston, 1965. ($3.95.) Paperback, New York: Avon, 1968. (95¢.)

A collection of contemporary prayers.

———. *Free to Live, Free to Die.* New York: Holt, Rinehart & Winston, 1967. ($3.95.) Paperback, New York: New American Library, 1968. (75¢.)

A collection of meditations on a wide-ranging field of subjects. Not like ordinary meditation books!

———. *Malcolm Boyd's Book of Days.* New York: Random House, 1968. ($4.95.) Paperback, Greenwich, Conn.: Fawcett World Library, 1969. (75¢.)

More and more of the same.

Coleman, Lyman. *Acts Alive, Man Alive,* and *Kaleidoscope.* Three mass media workbooks for a series of creative experiences to develop teens in living and loving the Christian way. Available from the Halfway House, Box 2, Newtown, Pennsylvania.

Habel, Norman C. *Are You Joking, Jeremiah?* St. Louis: Concordia, 1967. (Paperback, $1.25.)

A study of the Book of Jeremiah for teens.

———. *For Mature Adults Only.* Philadelphia: Fortress, 1969. (Paperback, $1.95.) Available also on a record, *For Mature Adults Only* (Joe Newman, Corky Hale, Robert Edwin), Fortress.

A book of poems and songs, with accompanying record; paeans of praise for a small group of teens with whom the author worked.

———. *Interrobang!* Philadelphia: Fortress, 1969. (Paperback, $1.95.)

A collection of poems, prayers, and litanies for all occasions.

———. *Wait a Minute, Moses!* St. Louis: Concordia, 1965. (Paperback, $1.25.)

A study of the book of Exodus for teens.

Richard S. Hanson, trans. *The Psalms in Modern Speech, For Public and Private Use.* 3 vols. Philadelphia: Fortress, 1968. (Paperback, $1.95 each, $5.50 a set.)

An alive new translation of the Psalms that follows the meter and captures the movement of the Hebrew poetry. The clearness of style and the division of each Psalm for responsive reading according to the Hebrew rubrics, provides greater insight into the Psalms and their contributions to contemporary worship.

Quoist, Michel. *Prayers.* New York: Sheed & Ward, 1963. ($3.95.)

A book of just about the most outstanding prayers you've ever read.

Sauer, Charles. *Heading for the Center of the Universe.* St. Louis: Concordia, 1965. (Paperback, $1.25.)

A study of the Lutheran liturgy in a different form, for teens.

SONGBOOKS AND FOLK MASSES

Create in Me, by Norman C. Habel. A folk mass written to the tunes of many familiar folk songs. Very lively. Available from Concordia Seminary Printshop, St. Louis, Mo., or a Lutheran Church Supply Store.

Hymnal for Young Christians. A massive collection of songs for all portions of the liturgy and for just general singing. Published by F. E. L. (Friends of the English Liturgy) Publications, a Roman Catholic publishing firm for liturgical work, this book is available at many denominational bookstores.

Hymns for Now, edited by Dean Kell. This is a good but limited collection of folk songs and folk hymns which will give a lot of mileage in contemporary worship services. Available either from the Youth Ministry Offices of the Lutheran Church—Missouri

Synod at 210 N. Broadway, St. Louis, Mo. or from your denominational bookstore.

Rejoice! A folk mass from within the context of the Episcopal church. The *Rejoice!* mass has become one of the most popular of the completely musical settings to the liturgy. It really moves. Available in three book sizes from your denominational bookstore.

Sing! Hymnal for Youth and Adults, edited by R. Harold Terry. Philadelphia: Fortress, 1970. Also available in a loose-leaf accompaniment edition. (*Sing!—Companion Recording,* 12-inch LP prepared as a teaching aid for this hymnal.)

An exciting selection, in a striking format. Gives background information on text and tune of hymn, and tells where to find it recorded.

Songs for Today, text by Ewald Bash and music by John Ylvisaker. An early production from the youth offices of the American Lutheran Church, this book contains mostly liturgical hymns and songs set to old folk tunes, plus a good collection of folk hymns and original material. A commentary pricks your mind with its questions about the meaning of the liturgy. This is an excellent beginning volume. Very inexpensive. Available from your denominational bookstore.

Songs from Notting Hill. A little book of songs from British sources in the contemporary worship vein. Available from your denominational bookstore.

Songs of Celebration. A fat collection of songs from the Center for Contemporary Worship in Chicago, a real powerhouse of creativity. There are many, many good things waiting for you when you open this one. Available from your denominational bookstore.

RECORDINGS OF CONTEMPORARY
WORSHIP SERVICES AND HYMNS

Cool Livin' (John Ylvisaker). Avant Garde. Modern songs by a real liturgically oriented poet. Available at most record stores.

Don't Cut the Baby in Half (John Ylvisaker). Avant Garde. Biblical stories set to music. Available at most stores.

Do You Know My Name? (Brother Juniper). Avant Garde. A celebration of life in music. Available at most stores.

Gonna Sing, My Lord (Joseph Wise). World Library of Sacred Music. Available at most stores.

I Know The Secret (Medical Mission Sisters). Avant Garde. Songs of celebration by eleven talented Roman Catholic sisters. Available at most stores.

Joy is Like the Rain (Medical Mission Sisters). Avant Garde. More songs. Available at most stores.

Knock Knock (Medical Mission Sisters). Avant Garde.

Join Hands, My Brothers (Gregory Miller). World Library of Sacred Music. Available at most stores.

Keep the Rumor Going (Robert Edwin). Avant Garde. Available at most stores.

Let the Cosmos Ring! A recording done by a creative Christian group called the Crosscurrents Community. Available from Crosscurrents Community, Apt. 111, 2301 Victoria Park Ave., Scarboro 734, Ontario, Canada.

Mass for Peace (The Berets). Avant Garde. An unusually good rock-and-roll mass, done by an Italian group in honor of the memory of Martin Luther King, Jr. Available at most stores.

Mass in F Minor (The Electric Prunes). Reprise. An early attempt at a rock-and-roll mass. Possibly no longer in stock, but available through most record stores.

Missa Laetare (composed by Edward V. Bonnemére; performed by the Philadelphia Seminary Choir under the direction of Robert Bornemann). Fortress. A mass that melds the Lutheran Liturgy with contemporary jazz. Available at your local store.

O Sing to the Lord a New Song (Joe Newman Jazz Quintet, with service led by the Rev. John Gensel). Fortress. A jazz mass. Available at your local store.

Praise the Lord in Many Voices (Robert Edwin). Avant Garde. A community mass. Available at your local store.

Rejoice! (H. Bruce Lederhouse). Scepter. Recording of the popular folk mass from the Episcopal tradition. If not available at your local store, write to Scepter Records, 254 W. 54th St., New York, N.Y.

Six Folk Masses for American Youth. World Library of Sacred Music. Quite a repertoire here! Available at your local store.

There's A Rhythm in Religion (Teen and Twenty). A good collection of joyful music. Available from Teen and Twenty Albums, Newberry Sound Studio, Ltd., 1356 Eglinton West, Toronto, Ontario, Canada.